In Memory of

MRS. J. B. HIGGINS, SR.

Mary and John Gray Library
Lamar University

DR. & MRS. ANDREW JOHNSON
donor

DISCARDED

PORTRAITS OF
MEXICAN BIRDS

PORTRAITS OF MEXICAN BIRDS

Fifty Selected Paintings

by George Miksch Sutton

Foreword by Enrique Beltrán

University of Oklahoma Press

Norman

By George Miksch Sutton

At a Bend in a Mexican River (New York, 1972)
High Arctic (New York, 1971)
Oklahoma Birds: Their Ecology and Distribution, with Comments on the Avifauna of the Southern Great Plains (Norman, 1967)
Iceland Summer: Adventures of a Bird Painter (Norman, 1961)
Mexican Birds: First Impressions (Norman, 1951)
Birds in the Wilderness (New York, 1936)
Eskimo Year (New York, 1934)
The Exploration of Southampton Island, Hudson Bay (Pittsburgh, 1932)
An Introduction to the Birds of Pennsylvania (Harrisburg, 1928)

Illustrated by George Miksch Sutton

The Birds of Colombia (in part) (by R. Meyer de Schauensee) (Narbeth, 1964)
The Birds of Arizona (by Allan Phillips, Joe Marshall, and Gale Monson) (Tucson, 1964)
Fundamentals of Ornithology (by Josselyn Van Tyne and Andrew J. Berger) (New York, 1959)
Georgia Birds (Norman, 1958)
A Guide to Bird Finding West of the Mississippi (by Olin Sewall Pettingill Jr.) (New York, 1953)
A Guide to Bird Finding East of the Mississippi (by Olin Sewall Pettingill Jr.) (New York, 1951)
World Book Encyclopedia (section on birds) (Chicago, 1941)
Birds of Western Pennsylvania (by W. E. C. Todd) (Pittsburgh, 1940)
The Golden Plover and Other Birds (by A. A. Allen) (Ithaca, 1939)
Wings, Fur and Shot (by Robert B. Vale) (Harrisburg, 1936)
American Bird Biographies (by A. A. Allen) (Ithaca, 1934)
The Birds of Minnesota (in part) (by T. S. Roberts) (Minneapolis, 1932)
The Burgess Seashore Book (in part) (by Thornton Burgess) (Boston, 1929)
The Birds of Florida (by H. H. Bailey) (Baltimore, 1925)
Our Bird Friends and Foes (by William Atherton Dupuy) (Philadelphia, 1925)

Publication of this volume has been made possible through a grant from The Wallace Thompson Fund of the University of Oklahoma Foundation.

Library of Congress Cataloging in Publication Data

Sutton, George Miksch, 1898-
    Portraits of Mexican birds.

1. Birds—Mexico—Pictorial works. I. Title.
QL686.S86   598.2'972   74-15911
ISBN 0-8061-1236-0

Copyright 1975 by the University of Oklahoma Press, Publishing Division of the University. Composed and printed at Norman, Oklahoma, U.S.A., by the University of Oklahoma Press. First edition.

May this collection of bird portraits honor the memory of Louis Agassiz Fuertes, whose halftone drawings in Florence Merriam Bailey's *Handbook of Birds of the Western United States* stirred me deeply when I was ten years old; whose criticism of my work while I was still in my teens made clear to me its good points and its bad; and whose unselfish offer to "show me just how he did it" took me to Sheldrake Point on Lake Cayuga in the summer of 1916. That summer in the maestro's shadow was the most important in my early life.

PRÓLOGO

En la literatura ornitológica mexicana existen algunas publicaciones que, además del indudable interés derivado de su contenido, se enriquecen también con planchas a colores que ilustran especies de nuestra rica y variada fauna.

La *Ornitología Mexicana* que Alfonso L. Herrera comenzó a publicar en 1898 en *La Naturaleza* y que continuó apareciendo en dicha revista hasta 1912, incluye láminas a colores de correcta ejecución.

Rafael Montes de Oca, en 1878, preparó una serie de 59 bellísimas acuarelas que representaban colibríes y orquídeas, que pensaba publicar con el largo titulo de *Monografía de los Colibríes i apuntes sobre las principales Orquídeas de México*. Desgraciadamente, los materiales quedaron inéditos durante largo tiempo, pues solo vieron la luz en 1963, en un volumen intitulado *Colibríes y Orquídeas de México*.

La más reciente adición es la hecha por Miguel Alvarez del Toro, cuya obra, *Aves de Chiapas* (1971), incluye la descripción de todas las especies hasta la fecha registradas en ese Estado, ilustradas con excelentes acuarelas, en su casi totalidad debidas al pincel del autor, y agrupadas en 81 láminas.

Junto a estos mexicanos—Herrera, Montes de Oca, Alvarez del Toro—ocupa lugar preferente un destacado ornitólogo norteamericano, George M. Sutton, que conjuga no sólo una gran capacidad científica mostrada infinidad de veces en sus escritos, sino que a la vez es un pintor de aves, digno de compararse con los mejores que en este campo existen o han existido.

Sus libros *Mexican Birds* (1951) y *At a Bend in a Mexican River* (1972) no sólo son interesantes por la información zoológica que ofrecen, sino también de agradable lectura por la forma en que el autor describe paisajes, comenta sucesos u ofrece opiniones. Además, las planchas a colores que los acompañan son de mérito indiscutible, deleitan la vista y obligan a lamentar que su número no sea mayor.

Gran parte de la obra pictórica de Sutton no ha sido aun dada a la publicidad, aunque se conoce a través de diversas exposiciones, de las que posiblemente la última, antes de la aparición de este libro, fué la que presentó en Colima.

Porque Sutton, y eso nos complace mucho a quienes nos honramos con su amistad de muchos años, ha estado siempre ligado a nuestro país, por los estudios realizados en materiales procedentes de México; la forma tan amable en que relata las impresiones de sus viajes por el territorio nacional; y la manera magistral en que ha dejado plasmada en colores la imagen de muchas de nuestras más bellas e interesantes aves.

Además, ha demostrado espíritu de compañerismo con sus colegas mexicanos, no solamente en el campo de la ornitología sino en otros lejanas a ella. Cuando en 1941 realizó una de sus expediciones ornitológicas por los estados de Nuevo León y Tamaulipas, pensé lo valioso que resultaría estudiar los protozoarios sanguíneos de los ejemplares colectados, dado que la competencia del colector aseguraba la precisión en las identificaciones de las especies. Y cuando tuve el atrevimiento de pedirle me proveyera de materiales no puso el menor reparo en hacerlo, y en abundancia llegaron a mis manos. Y eso que la tarea que le imponía no era nada sencilla, y requería tiempo que le robaba a otros trabajos más cercanos a sus intereses, pues no sólo le pedía frotis de sangre, sino también por aposición de cerebro, bazo, hígado y pulmón, tareas que requieren minucioso cuidado. Gracias a él pude publicar el primer trabajo mexicano sobre protozoarios parásitos de aves silvestres del país.

Hoy George M. Sutton vuelve a hacer otra gran contribución a la ornitología mexicana—posiblemente la más nutrida en láminas hasta la fecha—ya que en las páginas de este libro presenta 50 magníficas acuarelas, tan bellas estéticamente y perfectas desde el punto de visto zoológico, como todas las suyas, acompañadas de valiosas explicaciones in el texto. Su consulta resultará, al mismo tiempo que extraordinariamente útil como información, fuente de deleite con la contemplación de las pinturas.

Ojalá y el futuro nos depare todavía la dicha de ver reproducidas más láminas con las acuarelas de Sutton, tan valiosas para el artista como para el científico.

Enrique Beltrán
*Director, Institute for Mexican
Renewable Natural Resources*
University of Mexico

FOREWORD

In Mexican ornithological literature there exist some publications of decided interest because of their content that are also enriched with colorplates illustrating species of our rich and varied fauna.

The *Ornitología Mexicana* that Alfonso L. Herrera began to publish in 1898 in *La Naturaleza* and that continued to appear in said review until 1912, includes faultlessly executed colorplates.

In 1878, Rafael Montes de Oca prepared a series of 59 very beautiful watercolors representing hummingbirds and orchids that he thought of publishing with the long title of *Monografía de los Colibríes i apuntes sobre las principales Orquídeas de México*. Unfortunately, the materials remained unpublished for many years, only appearing in 1963, in a volume entitled *Colibríes y Orquídeas de México*.

The most recent addition is the work by Miguel Alvarez del Toro, whose *Aves de Chiapas* (1971) includes the description of all the species recorded to date in that state, illustrated with excellent watercolors, almost all from the brush of the author and grouped in 81 plates.

Beside these Mexicans—Herrera, Montes de Oca, Alvarez del Toro—a pre-eminent place is occupied by an outstanding North American ornithologist, George M. Sutton, whose great scientific ability has been demonstrated many times in his writings, and who, at the same time, is a bird artist worthy of comparison with the best ever in this field.

His books *Mexican Birds* (1951) and *At a Bend in a Mexican River* (1972) are interesting not only for the zoological information that they offer, but also for the pleasant way in which the author describes landscapes, comments on incidents, and offers opinions. Moreover, the accompanying colorplates are of incomparable quality, delighting the viewer and prompting him to exclaim that there are none better.

Much of Sutton's work has not yet been publicized, although his paintings have achieved recognition through several exhibitions, of which possibly the latest before the appearance of this book was the one presented in Colima.

Those of us who have been honored by his friendship for many years are greatly pleased that Sutton has always been bound to our country by his studies undertaken on materials originating from Mexico; his charming way of relating the impressions of his travels through the national territory; and the masterly way in which he has portrayed in color many of our most beautiful and interesting birds.

Besides, he has demonstrated a spirit of companionship with his Mexican colleagues not only in the field of ornithology but also in other related areas. When, in 1941, he was engaged in one of his ornithological expeditions through the states of Nuevo León and Tamaulipas, I thought how valuable it would be to study the sanguineous protozoans of the collected examples, since the competence of the collector assured precision in the identification of the species. And when I had the boldness to ask him to provide me with materials, he did not object, but sent them to me in abundance, although the task imposed upon him was difficult, requiring time that took him away from other works more closely related to his own interests. Furthermore, I asked him to secure not only blood smears, but also specimens of brains, spleens, livers, and lungs, a job which required meticulous care. Thanks to him I could publish the first Mexican work on parasitic protozoans of wild birds of the country.

Now George M. Sutton makes another great contribution to Mexican ornithology—possibly the richest in plates to date—since in the pages of this book he presents 50 magnificent watercolors, esthetically beautiful and perfect from the zoological point of view, and, as always, accompanied by valuable explanations in the text. His readers will discover an extraordinarily informative book and, at the same time, a fountain of delights in the contemplation of his paintings.

God grant that in the future we will be fortunate enough to see more of Sutton's paintings, as valuable for the artist as for the scientist.

Enrique Beltrán
*Director, Institute for Mexican
Renewable Natural Resources*
University of Mexico

PREFACE

The paintings reproduced in this book represent a time span of thirty-five years—1938 to 1973. All of them were made *in* Mexico, the earliest in the states of Nuevo León and Tamaulipas, the most recent in Colima. Those made in Tamaulipas in the spring and summer of 1941 were done largely indoors—at a built-in table in what might be called the "dining alcove" of the neat little one-storied, cement-floored house at the Rancho Rinconada on the banks of the lovely Río Sabinas. Those made in 1973 were done in the wonderfully pleasant patio at the main building of the Hacienda el Cóbano in Colima. The rest were done outdoors, invariably in the shade, for the glare from the white paper when struck by the sun was intolerable. Easels were made on the spot from saplings. To keep the big sheets of paper (each about 22 x 29 inches) flat and clean, I thumbtacked them to a plywood drawing board. In Tamaulipas I kept to the trails almost religiously, to avoid those wretched pests, the ticks. At high elevations in the mountains of Michoacán I worked in the middle of the day, since I could not manage pencil and brush with cold fingers.

The bird figures usually were drawn with unskinned specimens in hand, for in a finished "scientific skin" the feather patterns are sometimes distorted. Furthermore, in a dried skin the colors of the bill, feet, and eyelids invariably have faded. Eye-color I checked as carefully as possible with *living* birds. Eye-color is extremely difficult to catch, partly because it changes to some extent with the individual bird's mood, partly because when the pupil contracts, a pale ring often encircles it.

Let me thank those who helped with building easels, obtaining specimens, carrying equipment, bringing food and fresh drinking water, etc., especially the following: John B. Semple, Thomas D. Burleigh, Olin Sewall Pettingill Jr., Robert B. Lea, Dwain W. Warner, Ernest P. Edwards, Roger Hurd, Angel Lara, and Jenna Jo Hellack.

A final word about the paintbox that Louis Agassiz Fuertes gave me when I was eighteen years old. The box was old then; it is old and battered now. On the enamel inside, and still visible, are parts of the words "Payne's gray," written there in ink by Fuertes himself. I can't imagine tackling a bird drawing without having that old paintbox within touching distance.

Norman, Oklahoma George Miksch Sutton
January 23, 1975

CONTENTS

Prólogo by Enrique Beltrán _____ *page* *vii*
Foreword _____ *ix*
Preface _____ *xi*

THE PAINTINGS

Thicket Tinamou _____ *opposite page* 2
Bare-throated Tiger Heron _____ 4
Boat-billed Heron _____ 6
Muscovy Duck _____ 8
Bicolored Hawk _____ 10
Gray Hawk _____ 12
Ornate Hawk-Eagle _____ 14
Collared Forest Falcon _____ 16
Red-billed Pigeon _____ 18
Inca Dove _____ 20
White-fronted Dove _____ 22
Military Macaw _____ 24
Green Parakeet _____ 26
Yellow-headed Parrot _____ 28
Red-crowned Parrot _____ 30
Mangrove Cuckoo _____ 32
Squirrel Cuckoo _____ 34
Groove-billed Ani _____ 36
Northern Pygmy Owl _____ 38
Ferruginous Pygmy Owl _____ 40
Green-breasted Mango _____ 42
White-eared Hummingbird _____ 44
Green Violet-ear _____ 46
Mexican or Mountain Trogon _____ 48
Elegant Trogon _____ 50
Bar-tailed Trogon _____ 52
Blue-crowned Motmot _____ 54
Ringed Kingfisher _____ 56

Bronze-winged Woodpecker ——————————— *opposite page* 58
Ivory-billed Woodcreeper ————————————————————— 60
Masked Tityra ——————————————————————————— 62
Boat-billed Flycatcher ————————————————————— 64
Beardless Flycatcher ——————————————————————— 66
Magpie-Jay ————————————————————————————— 68
Brown Jay ——————————————————————————————— 70
Green Jay ——————————————————————————————— 72
Gray-barred Wren ———————————————————————— 74
Gray Silky ——————————————————————————————— 76
Peppershrike ——————————————————————————— 78
Chestnut-sided Shrike-Vireo ————————————————— 80
Tropical Parula Warbler ———————————————————— 82
Fan-tailed Warbler ——————————————————————— 84
Hooded Oriole ——————————————————————————— 86
Alta Mira Oriole ——————————————————————————— 88
Black-headed Oriole ————————————————————— 90
Abeille's Oriole ——————————————————————————— 92
Scrub Euphonia ——————————————————————————— 94
Red-throated Ant Tanager ——————————————————— 96
Black-headed Saltator ————————————————————— 98
Blue Bunting ——————————————————————————— 100
A Word from the Author ————————————————————— 103

PORTRAITS OF MEXICAN BIRDS

THICKET TINAMOU

The tinamous—those terrestrial "partridges" of Mexico, Central America, and South America—are for me among the world's wonder-birds. They have good wings, but rarely fly. Some of them lay eggs whose gaudy colors and glossiness remind me of Christmas tree ornaments. I have become well acquainted with only one of the forty-five known species, the northernmost of them all, the Thicket Tinamou (*Crypturellus cinnamomeus*). Because I have crawled along trails on hands and knees, forced my way through savagely barbed, all but impenetrable tangles of *huapilla* (wild pineapple), got myself covered with those despicable tiny ticks called *pinolillos*, climbed trees convinced that I would surely see the birds if only I could look *down* into their mat-covered habitat—in short, because I have shed blood, suffered aches and pains, and endured humiliation day after day over them *and finally got one*, I feel as if the world's whole population of Thicket Tinamous is peculiarly mine. Funny isn't it, how possessive a man can feel over something that isn't his at all!

The trouble was that we could hear the secretive birds calling near and far. There were literally scores of them in the broad floodplain of the Sabinas. Their call was a mellow, slightly quavering, slightly interrogative, whistled *Whoo-ee-you*? We heard it along every trail at river-level. We heard it below us when we climbed the big foothill west of the river. We heard it while we were working or resting inside the house at the Rancho Rinconada. We could not get away from it. "Who are you?" it seemed to ask. "What right have you to be here? This habitat is ours, remember. We belong here—and you don't!"

Never shall I forget my first look at a living wild tinamou. The date was March 4, 1938. I was on one of the many trails that the *paisanos* had cut through the dense *huapilla*. When I stood or crouched motionless, tinamous began calling all about me. So close were some of them that I could hear their footfalls on the dead leaves. Circumstance forced me to shift attention occasionally—now to a flock of Military Macaws whose squawks made my spine tingle, now to a band of Scrub Euphonias passing low overhead, now to the tinkling song of a White-bellied Wren, a species I did not know well. I didn't quite forget the tinamous, but the singing of one of these wrens close by reminded me that we needed a specimen. I lifted the gun, waited for the tiny, stub-tailed bird to come into view, and shot—realizing at that very instant that my target had moved out of sight, back of one of the tough, jagged leaves.

Into the thicket I plunged, hoping that I might have got the bird after all. Looking carefully, I found shot-marks all over the leaves of the plant at which I had aimed. The pattern of marks was dense. If I had hit the wren at all, I had probably killed it. Confident that I'd find the specimen if only I looked hard enough, I began moving the great saw-edged leaves of one great rosette, holding them back with my left hand while lifting them one by one with my right. The lowest leaf was dry, partly dead, and hard to move. I lifted it and there, crouching on the ground not more than 4 feet from my very face, looking at me with wide-open grayish-yellow eyes, was—a tinamou!

What opportunity was there for letting the armful of *huapilla* go and grabbing up the gun? The opportunity perhaps, but not the impulse. Out shot the brown bird as if catapulted. Straight through the tangle it flew on roaring wings, barely clearing the sharp tips of the *huapilla* plants and coming noisily to earth thirty yards away. The whole performance—the takeoff, the panic-stricken bolt through the vines, the awkward landing—all this was the escape of a creature that knew nothing of steering a course or putting on brakes in flight; the getaway of a virtually tail-less bird so essentially terrestrial that it might never in its whole life have flown before!

BARE-THROATED TIGER HERON

Not far north of Victoria, the capital city of Tamaulipas, is a quiet stream whose banks are lined with big trees, the Río Corona, a major tributary of the Soto la Marina. Back a way from the river and trees is thicket much like that which the traveler sees along so much of the northernmost stretch of the Laredo–Mexico City highway. The big trees, forming a fringe on each bank and thus enclosing the river, are a world apart—a sort of finger of the New World tropics reaching northward. In this narrow world live parrots of two species, strange birds of prey known as forest falcons and crane-hawks, and two big tropical woodpeckers whose superficial likeness to each other furnishes biologists an excellent example of "convergent evolution." A bird student fresh from the north and new to the tropics is awed by these woods, this river world, for it is all so very different from anything he has experienced. The sparkling green that he sees is that of parrots, wild, free-flying parrots. It is a green that is incredibly rich and bright. He pinches himself to make sure that he is awake. So much of what he sees and hears is like a dream.

One of the handsomest of the "new" birds along the Corona is the Bare-throated Tiger Heron (*Tigrisoma mexicanum*), a species that ranges along both Atlantic and Pacific coastal slopes in Mexico southward from central Tamaulipas and southern Sonora to northwestern Colombia. It is considerably the more northward-ranging of the two tiger herons found in the New World, the other being the Lineated Tiger Heron (*T. lineatum*), a species with white, fully-feathered throat found in Central and South America (Honduras to northern Argentina). The name "tiger heron" describes the young of both species rather well, but not the adult of either. The young are boldly barred with black and light reddish brown.

John Semple, Tom Burleigh, and I did not see much of the Bare-throated Tiger Heron along the Corona during our stay in that area in 1938, but I shall never forget the surprise I felt as one of the strange birds flew up almost from underfoot at the water's edge, squawked loudly, and alighted in a tree. Another surprise awaited me that day: the oddly beautiful, somewhat reptilian, pale greenish yellow of the unfeathered throat. I painted the head and neck of the bird that day (February 19). This painting first appeared as Plate VIII in my book *Mexican Birds* (1951) as Cabanis's Tiger-Bittern, the name by which it was known at that time.

A bit later—on February 24—while I was standing quietly among shrubbery close to the river, an immature tiger heron glided slowly past, obviously quite unaware of my presence, alighting not more than 20 feet away behind the bole of a big cypress. A plan quickly resolved itself in my mind: I would lay aside gun, collecting creel, and binocular and creep up to see how close I could get. Completely hidden by the great trunk, I could not see the bird until, now on all fours, I moved a little to the right. There stood the heron, on one of the cypress's knees, preening a wing. It was only about 5 feet away. When it saw my outstretched hand, then my arm, then *me*, it flapped clumsily off, squawking as if in mortal agony.

In the spring of 1941 our four-man party did not often see the Bare-throated Tiger Heron along the Río Sabinas, in southwestern Tamaulipas, but on May 1, Bob Lea found a nest on an almost horizontal branch about 50 feet above the water in a huge, moss-hung cypress. Alas, we never learned what was in that nest, though Sewall Pettingill photographed one of the adults walking toward it.

BOAT-BILLED HERON

One of the strangest birds I have ever painted is the Boat-bill (*Cochlearius cochlearius*), a New World heron found in low country from Tamaulipas in the east and Sinaloa in the west southward through Mexico, Central America, and South America as far as Bolivia and northern Argentina. A nocturnal creature, it is much like a night heron in many ways. Indeed the late Adriaan van Rossem called the Boat-bills that he observed in El Salvador "curious travesties of the black-crowned night heron [*Nycticorax nycticorax*]." Concerning them he wrote: "They feed singly either by night or by day in the shallow waters of lake shores, along rivers, and in marshes and usually roost in companies, very often in association with black-crowned night herons. Like many other herons the boat-bills have excellent night vision; in fact a good proportion of their hunting is done after dark. As noted previously [in an article in a leading ornithological journal] there is no reflection from their eyes, a circumstance which appears in no way to affect their powers of nocturnal vision" (1938, Field Mus. Zool. Ser., 23: 84-85).

The Boat-bill breeds colonially. A colony of about twenty pairs that van Rossem found at Lake Guija in El Salvador were nesting in a single large tree that overhung a small, deep, alligator-infested pool formed by the overflow from a creek entering the lake. The nests resembled those of night herons. The birds were extremely tame; "for the most part the sitting birds could not be frightened into flight by guns fired under the tree, though at each shot they burst into a wild jumble of squawking and gabbling which lasted for several seconds" (van Rossem, *op. cit.*, 85).

I well remember my first wild Boat-bill—not a living bird, alas, but a fine specimen shot by Robert B. Lea and brought to me literally within moments after its death. I had been at work that day on a small bird whose species-custom it was to eat the leaves of a certain shrubby nightshade. The bird in my picture had turned out fairly well, but try as I did to make the nightshade leaves look soft and woolly, I could not get the effect I wanted. In my determination to make them look right I went so far as to erase and re-do them, but they continued to look leathery rather than woolly.

The afternoon was waning. The bench was becoming intolerably hard, the light poor, my patience thin. I had half-decided to take the drawing to the yard and burn it in a fine Audubonesque display of indignation, when what should I hear but the slamming of the back door, quick sloshy footfalls, and Bob Lea's voice, blurting out, "Wait till you see what I've got this time, Doc! I shot it down the river and brought it right in so you could paint it. It looks like a funny heron of some sort."

The enthusiastic Bob, breathing hard, handed me the Boat-bill. It was all beak, head, and neck, with floppy wings and pale green legs hanging on somehow. Its large dark eyes had not yet quite closed. Fascinated by its almost reptilian visage, the queer shades of yellow on its naked face, and the delicate bloom on its plumage, I let myself admire it a moment, then, stepping outside to rest my eyes, and rubbing myself as my baboon forebears must have before their fancy seat-pads evolved, went to work again.

That picture I never finished. I painted the bill and the great doleful eye with care and dashed in the plumage, but by the time I was ready to tackle the network of scales on the legs, darkness had come, Sewall Pettingill was lighting the kerosene lamp, and Dwain Warner, with lips smacking, was announcing turtle stew.

So here is my picture. Whatever its shortcomings, it may nevertheless be the only watercolor sketch ever made by man of a freshly collected Boat-bill.

MUSCOVY DUCK

As a barnyard fowl the Muscovy Duck (*Cairina moschata*) is not at all prepossessing. Usually its plumage is white or white with black patches here and there. The bare skin at the base of the bill and about the eyes appears to be covered with warts. Swimming, it may be graceful enough, but on shore it has a squat, flabby, almost degenerate appearance.

What a different creature is the wild Muscovy! The same in general shape, of course, but with truly sprightly gait if it happens to be walking across a gravel bar along its wild tropical river. Behold the subtly iridescent, almost velvety black plumage, the bold white patch in each wing, and the jaunty, turned-to-one-side crest of the drake! A truly fine bird he is. The hen is only about half as heavy. She has no conspicuous crest and she is less iridescent of plumage, but she, too, is handsome.

I became acquainted with the wild Muscovy along the Río Sabinas, south of old Ciudad Victoria, in the spring of 1938. My first glimpse was memorable. Intent on reaching certain big *jobo* plum trees before sunup, I had set out in the dark and was wading a shallow part of the river, a stretch that we called "the riffles," when two big birds flew over me. They were almost within touching distance, yet all I could see was their big dark forms against the sky. The sound of their rapidly beating wings was almost frightening. *They must be some kind of goose*, I thought, they were so big. Then I recalled that Mr. Bensel had told us about Muscovies. "Yes indeed they are here," he had said. "The Mexican name for them is *pato real*. That means royal duck."

Certain facts about Muscovies greatly surprised me. I saw them almost every day, invariably along the river, usually in pairs or singly, never in flocks. When I happened upon them they flew not up from the water, as I'd expected they would, but out from big horizontal branches that reached over the river's edge. They were arboreal. So fond of certain branches were they that I could count on finding them there and seeing them well if I approached cautiously. On examining the specimen whose head I painted, I discovered that the claws were strong and sharp—big enough to be of considerable help in perching. Another notable feature was the pupil, which was not circular but elliptical.

Our Mexican friends told us that the *pato real* did not nest until after the floods, later in the summer. The several eggs were to be looked for in a natural cavity in a big tree, often above water. We were far too early that season for a nest. The reproductive organs of specimens that we examined were not even slightly enlarged. In 1941 my companions and I saw small flocks of Muscovies as late as April 14, but only pairs and single birds after that. Occasionally we witnessed courtship behavior. A courting drake swam about the female slowly, wagging his tail, thrusting his head far forward and drawing it back slowly, uttering throaty grunts, or pursued her in flight, keeping close behind or to one side, calling amorously.

BICOLORED HAWK

In my collection are two specimens of the handsome short-winged, long-tailed tropical bird of prey known as the Bicolored Hawk (*Accipiter bicolor*), a non-migratory species that ranges from southern Tamaulipas and eastern San Luis Potosí southward to Peru and Brazil. Each of the two specimens is an adult female. One was shot not far from the hill village of Gómez Farías in southwestern Tamaulipas, by a Mexican nicknamed "Cuckoo," and prepared by my friend William B. Heed, who is now on the faculty of the University of Arizona. The other I obtained myself in eastern San Luis Potosí.

How I wish I had been with "Cuckoo" when he got his specimen! The date was August 16, 1950, the spot a wild gully on the foothill about 2 kilometers west of a shallow, gravel-bottomed stretch of the Río Sabinas used by the Mexicans as a ford and called by them Paño Ayuctle. A party with dogs had cornered and killed a full-grown *tigre* (a jaguar, *Felis onca*) the day before, and Bill Heed, knowing that the skull of the big cat was just as valuable scientifically as the skin, had insisted that the carcass be found and the precious head removed. As the two of them were proceeding with their work, a hawk unlike any Bill had ever seen came flying in close to the ground, obviously curious as to what was going on, or intent upon obtaining another meal at the *tigre* carcass. As it swept upward to a perch close by, Bill noted its over-all grayness and the striking rufous-brown of its tibial feathers of "flags." Its tarsi and toes were yellow, but the cere was dark, of a vague color not strikingly different from that of the bill.

I collected my specimen on January 5, 1952, on a trail leading from our camp at Sabinal to the remote little village of Osmalón. A good friend and former graduate student, Richard R. Graber, was with me. We had been moving quietly through the forest, never for an instant free of the feeling that we were intruders, vandals of a sort, disturbers of the profound peace. The tops of the trees were so far above us that small patches of sky seemed not one bit farther away than the leaves. Occasionally we stopped, made a squeaking sound kissing the back of a hand, and waited, motionless, to see what curious creature would appear. There weren't many small birds at our level in the understory—an ant tanager or two, a hummingbird, perhaps a woodcreeper. At one spot a Bicolored Hawk dashed in, circled us closely—giving us an unforgettable look at its fanned-wide, boldly barred gray-and-black tail—and alighted, glaring at us with its orange eyes.

Let no one think that the branch in my drawing was "any old branch" picked up at camp. It was carried back to camp from the spot at which the hawk was shot. I am not sure that it was from an oak. We did shoot a twig from one of the high trees and found among the leaves beautiful mahogany-red acorn cups. Would that I had painted them too, but the hawk had perched not near the end of a branch where leaves and acorns were, but in toward the heart of the tree.

The specimen's tarsi, toes, and eyelids were bright yellow, but the cere was dark greenish gray. In both Bill Heed's specimen and mine the ovary was paired, a condition found widely in the short-winged, long-tailed bird-hawks of the genus *Accipiter*.

GRAY HAWK

A well-known raptorial bird of Mexican lowlands is the Gray Hawk (*Buteo nitidus*), a middle-sized species that ranges northward into the United States a short way beyond the border and southward through Central and South America to northern Argentina. In my opinion the bird's common name is inexcusably dull. To be sure, adults of both sexes are gray above and finely barred with gray below, but the color, which has a special light-catching quality, deserves a far more exciting word than *gray*. The scientific name *nitidus*, meaning *shining*, is better. This I have sensed on many occasions, especially when I have seen the bird perched quietly on a dead branch not in the very top of a tree but halfway up, well above ground or water, its underparts gleaming in the morning sunlight. Even at considerable distance the bright yellow of the cere and mouth-corners seems to sparkle.

Memorable indeed were two "shining" hawks that I watched for a quarter of an hour as they circled above the Río Sabinas in the spring of 1941. When I first saw them they were not far above the treetops. One was perceptibly larger than the other, and both were squealing. After they had circled upward to a thousand feet or so, the smaller bird, the male, began swooping. Starting from a point well above the female, he suddenly folded his wings, headed downward, shot past his mate at great speed, spread his wings and swooped upward, upward, upward until he was well above her once more. Here, after circling twice, he swooped again, barely missing her. There was no looping the loop, but it was almost that. How the exuberance of that male bird declared itself! How "dawn the rosy-fingered" touched his lovely underwings as he rushed upward! Whether the female was impressed or not, most certainly I was.

Much that I have read about the Gray Hawk gives the impression that its food is largely insects, small reptiles, and other "lowly" forms of life; but I know from repeated observation that it is a confirmed catcher of small birds. One day while I was at work not far from the river I heard the snapping of a branch, a sharp thud, and a heart-rending shriek as a Gray Hawk snatched an oriole from a branch and bore it off. The whole episode took place only a few yards overhead. The sound of that futile shrieking stayed with me for days. I knew full well that the oriole was done for, but it continued to proclaim its agony as long as life lasted.

My drawing, made on March 31, 1941, shows a male bird perched on a bamboo stalk. Wanting to show prey of some sort in one of the yellow feet, I asked everyone at the Rancho Rinconada to "catch something for the hawk to eat" while I went ahead with my work. Instantly there was a frantic scrambling outside the house. Bob Lea and Dwain Warner shouted and little Ramón Rodriguez screamed. What they brought was a fine, slender lizard, quite unharmed. I didn't want to kill it, partly because we all liked having lizards around the house and partly because I wanted to be sure that the colors would be those of just such a freshly-killed lizard as the hawk would be carrying. So I put the lizard to sleep with a whiff of carbon tetrachloride. When I had finished drawing it, I took it outdoors, put it on a windowsill in the sun, and watched it "come to life" and whisk up the screen.

ORNATE HAWK-EAGLE

One of the New World's handsomest birds of prey is the Ornate Hawk-Eagle (*Spizaetus ornatus*), a boldly marked, conspicuously crested inhabitant of heavy woodland from Tamaulipas southward through Central and South America to Peru, Paraguay, and northern Argentina. Although chiefly a lowland species, it has been recorded at elevations up to 5,000 feet.

I have seen the bird chiefly in southwestern Tamaulipas, where it is uncommon. Three experiences come instantly to mind when I think of it. I first saw it one foggy morning while climbing a steep, slippery trail leading up the foothill to the "red rocks." For no obvious reason I paused to look about me. On glancing upward I saw a large bird of prey perched on a dead stub directly above me. It was peering at me with golden-yellow eyes, obviously curious, though it did not bob its head as hawks often do when "sizing something up" from two angles. It was standing on one foot, perfectly at ease. As I lifted my binocular for a close look, one foot came slowly down from the fluffed belly plumage and the long crest, which looked like a single feather, rose to a vertical position.

Soon after the hawk-eagle flew off, a tree to one side came suddenly to life, water showered down from the agitated leaves, and a flock of parrots flew out, shrieking wildly. It was they the hawk-eagle had been after. So motionless had they been that I might have looked straight at them without realizing they were there. Now that the graver danger had withdrawn, they were getting away from me!

Later that morning—even before I knew what the big birds were—I observed a pair of hawk-eagles. Both kept up a thin, clear screaming, though neither dived at me. The male, which was considerably the smaller, carried around a partly eaten mammal of some sort, probably a squirrel. The female I collected, finding a green parrot feather clinging to one bloody claw.

Three days later, farther up on the same foothill, I was puzzled by a sound of snapping twigs upslope a few rods. Looking that way, I saw a big bird of prey heading straight for me. This time I was in a quandary. If I was being attacked, some move was certainly in order. Should I shoot? At that instant a quail roared out from underfoot and off through the brush. After it dashed the predator, a hawk-eagle, which almost struck me as it changed course abruptly, set its wings for another stoop, and crashed through the vines. I had no idea where the poor quail was—whether on the ground or still flying—but I heard branches breaking and saw dead leaves whirling. The whole encounter was so swift, and the sequence of events so unpredictable, that I did not catch up properly with its beginning before it had ended. Walking in the direction I had seen quail and pursuer take, I looked carefully for evidence of capture, but found neither scattered feathers nor blood. What I pondered as I stood there, what I have pondered many times since, was the terrific singleness of purpose I had witnessed, the utter abandonment of caution, the swift action.

On March 22, 1949, on a shoulder of that same foothill, well above river-level, I heard the thin, somewhat musical squealing of an Ornate Hawk-Eagle. For a time I thought the sounds were coming from a young Hooded Grosbeak (*Hesperiphona abeillei*) in the top of a tall liquidambar. The fluffy little bird sat there, probably waiting for food. Over and over I heard the squeal, but the grosbeak did not even open its mouth. It dawned on me at last that the squeals were coming from far, far above the grosbeak—from somewhere in the sky. Then I saw the hawk-eagle, identified it from its big, boldly barred tail, and watched its graceful soaring. What an impressive creature it was!

COLLARED FOREST FALCON

The long-tailed, short-winged, ruff-faced bird of prey currently known as the Collared Forest Falcon (*Micrastur semitorquatus*) ranges from northern South America northward through Central America to the Mexican states of Sinaloa, San Luis Potosí, and Tamaulipas. I had my first look at the species along the Río Corona near the village of Güemes, Tamaulipas, on February 28, 1938. In some ways that look was the best I have ever had, for the bird was perched in a tree only a few yards from the one I was in. The situation deserves explanation.

I had shot a small bird whose lifeless body had caught on a thorn about 15 feet up. From the ground, I could not tell whether the carcass was impaled or merely lodged between thorn and twig, but throwing sticks and stones only seemed to ensconce the specimen more firmly, so up I went. The ascent was difficult because of the thorns. As I climbed, a noisy mob of jays and other small birds gathered. Having lifted my specimen from the thorn and tossed it carefully to an open space on the ground, I was starting downward when the outcry of the small birds suddenly stopped. Wondering why the silence, I looked about. Every one of the jays, orioles, and other little birds had departed. Instead of them, on a branch at about my level, was a Collared Forest Falcon. The handsome creature was looking not at me but at my specimen, and its plan was plain enough. Needless to say, I swung from the nearest branch I could reach and dropped to the ground. I did not get there an instant too soon. The thwarted falcon gave a strange cry as it shot past me and off through the woods.

That day I made a watercolor sketch of the head of a Collared Forest Falcon that another member of our party had shot. The eyes of the bird were dark brown, nearly black. The bony shield above the eye, a notable feature in many birds of prey, was not pronounced, nor were the colors of the eyelids, cere, and mouth-corners very bright. Most surprising of all was the shortness of the leg feathers. All the "true" falcons of the world have long tibial feathers that are called the "flag," but in these forest falcons the tibial feathers are very short.

So definitely a creature of the woods is *Micrastur semitorquatus* that it doesn't often fly above the treetops. Never have I seen it circling overhead, even on a bright sunny day. When it forages it keeps low. It often captures that fellow inhabitant of the chaparral, the chachalaca, a galliform bird that it oddly resembles in size and proportions.

In the spring of 1941, along the Río Sabinas, I watched a pair of Collared Forest Falcons obtaining prey. Attracted by the outcry of small birds, I ran from the house in time to see one falcon flying laboriously through the brush about 6 feet from the ground dragging a big, live snake. The struggling reptile broke free, but on reaching the ground it was pinned down by the falcon's mate, grasped by powerful talons, and once more carried. Falcons and writhing prey were escorted into the depths of the thicket by the clamorous cortege. From the cries of the small birds I could not tell whether they were angered by the presence of the falcons or pleased by the departure of the snake.

What do I remember most vividly about the Collared Forest Falcon? Perhaps its rapid wingbeats as it dashes through the brush; perhaps its ability to run if it needs to in capturing prey; perhaps its doleful cries, given at times in duet, just before nightfall. No wonder that it was sometimes called the "moan-bird."

RED-BILLED PIGEON

The Red-billed Pigeon (*Columba flavirostris*) — a not very well-named bird, since only the basal part of the bill is red and the color is not conspicuous — ranges from southern Texas in the east and central Sonora in the west, southward through the coastal lowlands of Mexico and Central America as far as central Costa Rica. Throughout this area, which includes the whole of the Yucatán Peninsula, it is well known and locally common. It is about the size of a domestic pigeon and the flapping of its wings as it flies up from the wild river's edge calls a barnyard to mind. Like all pigeons and doves with which I am familiar, it is very dependent on water. When it drinks it sticks its head half under, for its bill is rather short.

I have seen little of the Red-billed Pigeon in the Lower Río Grande Valley, but along rivers in Tamaulipas, San Luis Potosí, and Veracruz I have seen it in great numbers. Along the Corona on February 18, 1938, I watched great flocks as they fed on mistletoe berries. Certain big trees were fairly covered with the parasite and here the pigeons gathered literally by the hundreds, hurtling down from the sky, and then, after turning sharply, swooping upward toward the branches, where alighting required adroit maneuvering with wings and tail. There was nothing reticent about their behavior. Their arrival, alighting, and gobbling of berries all was noisy. Frequently they sparred for choice positions, knocking each other about with blows from their lifted wings.

The impression created early that morning was that every Red-billed Pigeon of the countryside was interested in nothing but food. Once their crops were filled, however, the flocks idled in the tops of dead trees, flew down to gravel-bars for a long drink, or scattered through the woods. As a rule they alighted well up from the ground in large trees, most of which were close to the river. Here the amorous males cooed persistently, standing with heads up and chests bulging, calling *coooooo, up, cup-a-cooooooo*, each long syllable swelling, then dying down. Heard close at hand, the cooing had a rough, breathy quality. Pairs must have been forming throughout the area that day.

Along the Río Sabinas in the spring of 1941 we noted the first sign of nest-building on March 18. On that date Robert Lea watched a bird carrying a twig in its bill. In the same area in late May, 1947, I observed a displaying bird flying in wide circles on slowly beating wings — behavior I had not noted in earlier years. On May 16, 1947, Ernest Edwards found a nest about 30 feet up in a large cypress near the river at Paño Ayuctle. We were not sure what was in that nest. On May 21, 1947, I found a nest holding one egg in a small tree only 6 feet up, about 15 feet from the river's edge. Here the incubating bird flapped and fluttered noisily, and occasionally *growled*, when leaving the nest. The egg started to hatch three days later, but on May 25 we found the partly hatched chick dead in the nest.

My painting, made near the Sabinas in the spring of 1941, shows a mated pair of the handsome birds. Note especially the strangely shaped head and the red in the basal half of the bill.

INCA DOVE

The trim, delicately marked *tortolita* or Inca Dove (*Scardafella inca*) is very Mexican, though not by any means exclusively so. It ranges northward as far as central Texas, southern New Mexico, and southern Arizona, and southward to northernmost Costa Rica. There appears to be a gap in this extensive range, for it has not been reported from the southeastern Mexican states of Tlaxcala, Tabasco, Campeche, and Yucatán. I have seen it chiefly in Tamaulipas and Colima. Though commonest in low country, it has been recorded at elevations up to 7,800 feet. In the fine city of Cuernavaca, Morelos, where I frequently saw it during a recent visit there, its softly hooted *no hope* was the first bird call that I identified to my complete satisfaction.

I cannot insist that anyone interested in birds must surely go to Santa Rosa, a village not far northeast of Monterrey, Nuevo León, for profound changes may have taken place there with the passing of time, but I remember that *poblado*—as I saw it on February 1, 1938—as the "birdiest" I had ever visited. Mixed flocks of blackbirds flying up and away were so dense that they obliterated whole rows of pink and blue housefronts. Hardly a building was without vultures on its roof, most of them the black-all-over species called the *zopilote* by the Mexicans. Perched in almost every tree was a comfortable looking big hawk. And whole patches of ground were hidden by doves—Inca Doves and Ground Doves (*Columbina passerina*) chiefly, but a few Mourning Doves (*Zenaida macroura*) too. Mankind has long considered the dove a symbol of peace, but those Santa Rosa doves, especially the two smaller species, were as unabashedly quarrelsome as any birds I have ever watched. Part of the trouble was, of course, that every dove was hungry and every feeding area circumscribed, so fully half of the energies of the broad-backed little birds was expended in shoving each other out of the way and in dealing good stiff blows with lifted wings. Watching the turmoil was fascinating. The swirling and eddying held the attention as the waters of a rapid do.

In our yard at the Rancho Rinconada in southwestern Tamaulipas the Inca Doves became very tame. On wet mornings before egg-laying started the pairs sat side by side, not a comfortable distance apart but jammed against each other tightly, headed in the same direction with feathers so fluffed out as to make them appear to be one rather oddly shaped bird rather than two.

My drawing was started in the town of Mante, Tamaulipas. There, while waiting for Ernest Edwards and his party to join me, I drew the branches of a flowering flamboyant tree or royal poinciana. My chief problem was the hundreds of small caterpillars whose droppings continued to fall on the paper. A good share of my time was used in lifting these carefully off with a knife blade and erasing thoroughly. The two birds, a male and female, I added later.

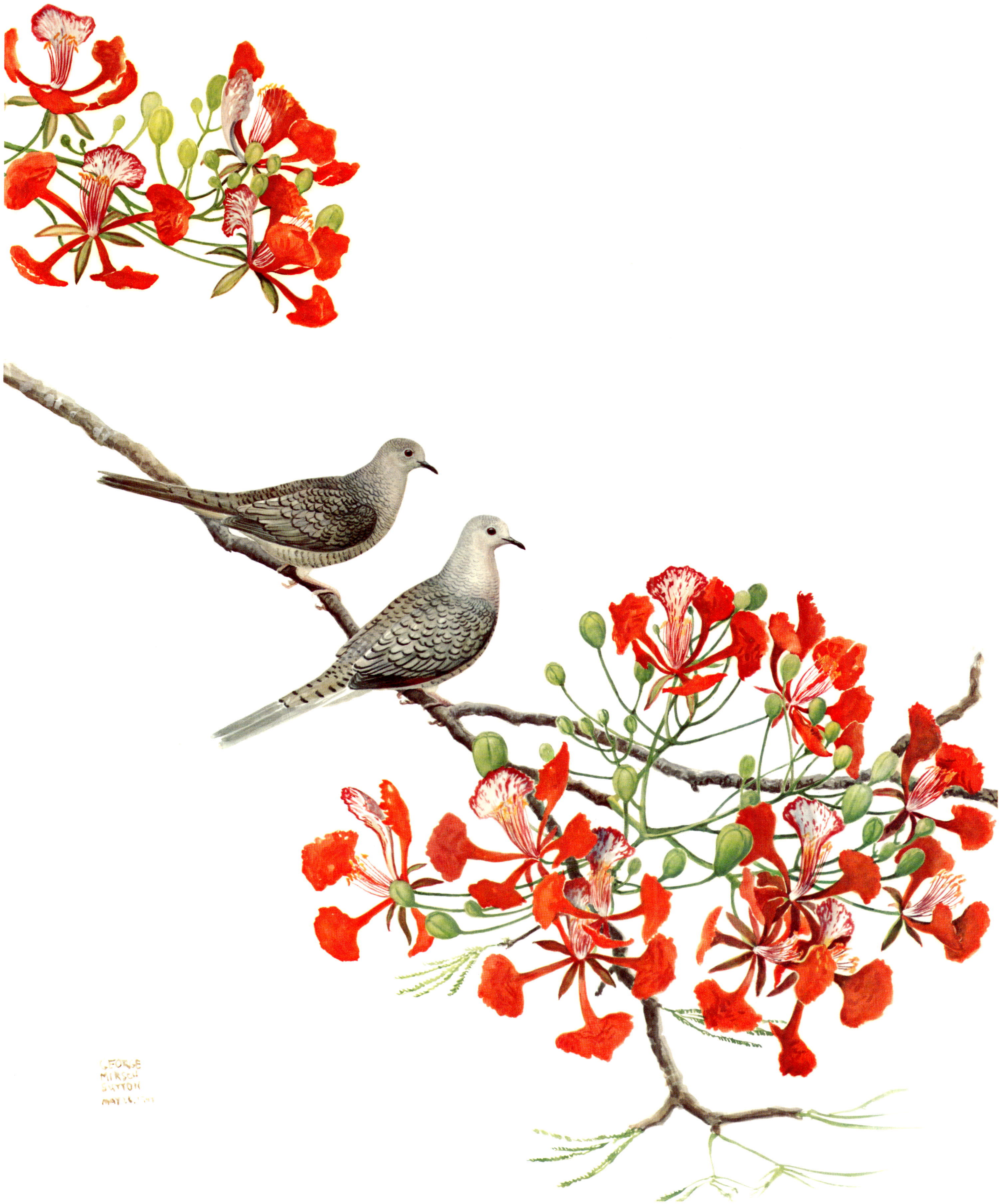
GEORGE
MIKSCH
SUTTON

WHITE-FRONTED DOVE

The White-fronted Dove (*Leptotila verreauxi*), sometimes called the White-tipped Dove, is a ground-loving bird of dense thickets in dry brushland. It is a species of very wide range, being found throughout coastal lowlands from southern Texas in the east and southern Sonora in the west southward through Mexico (including the Yucatán Peninsula), Central America, and South America as far as Argentina. It is not quite as long as the well-known Mourning Dove (*Zenaida macroura*), but larger-bodied, and it has a rounded rather than pointed tail.

Along the Río Corona in central Tamaulipas I became well acquainted with some of the White-fronted Dove's ways on February 18, 1938. Since forcing my way through the brush was painful and noisy, I kept to the riverbed that morning, wading where the water was shallow and clambering up to higher ground where the channel came close to shore. Every time I left the riverbed I put up one or more fair-sized birds that I felt sure were doves, though I flushed several before getting a good look at one. They flew up, usually one at a time, occasionally two or three together, from half-hidden pools, darted swiftly back into the thicket, and alighted with a whirring of wings and a scattering of dust and dry leaves. Peering cautiously over the bank, I sometimes saw one only a rod or so away, walking rapidly off with head bobbing at each step, or standing on a fallen branch with body quite motionless but with head jerking as if in an effort to see me more clearly and tail moving slowly up and down. This part of the river's flood-plain was so dimly lighted and the brush so thick that I rarely saw more than part of a bird at any one time. The fieldmarks that I finally came to depend on were the rufous of the underwing, which showed in flight, and the widely fanned tail, whose middle pair of feathers was about the same color as the back and whose outer pairs were dark with white tipping. Not until I had obtained a specimen did I see the pink and pale blue of the bare skin in front of and around the eye and the exquisite rainbow iridescence on the sides of the neck.

I heard the soft, long-drawn-out cooing of the species long before realizing that I was hearing anything. This sounds like an attempt to be clever, but the statement is valid. So vague was the cooing, so like a sound the wind might make, that I heard it over and over without paying the slightest attention to it. Then, "as luck would have it," I *saw* a bird cooing and suddenly realized that the mellifluous organpoint that I had been half-aware of all morning was from White-fronted Doves. There must have been literally hundreds of the doves in the broad flood-plain of the Corona.

Along the Sabinas in the spring of 1941 the White-fronted Dove was less common than it had been along the Corona, but we heard it every day and saw it not only in the chaparral between river and highway but also in the heavy woods on the foothill west of the river. We found several nests, those on the foothill being on the ground among boulders, those at river-level a few feet up in trees or vines. Two nests discovered March 29 each held two heavily incubated eggs. At one nest both eggs hatched the following day. A nest found as late as April 15 held fresh eggs. At a nest under the corner of a big rock on the foothill, Sewall Pettingill took appealing motion pictures of the parent bird pumping up food for the two little squabs, one at each side of the old bird's mouth.

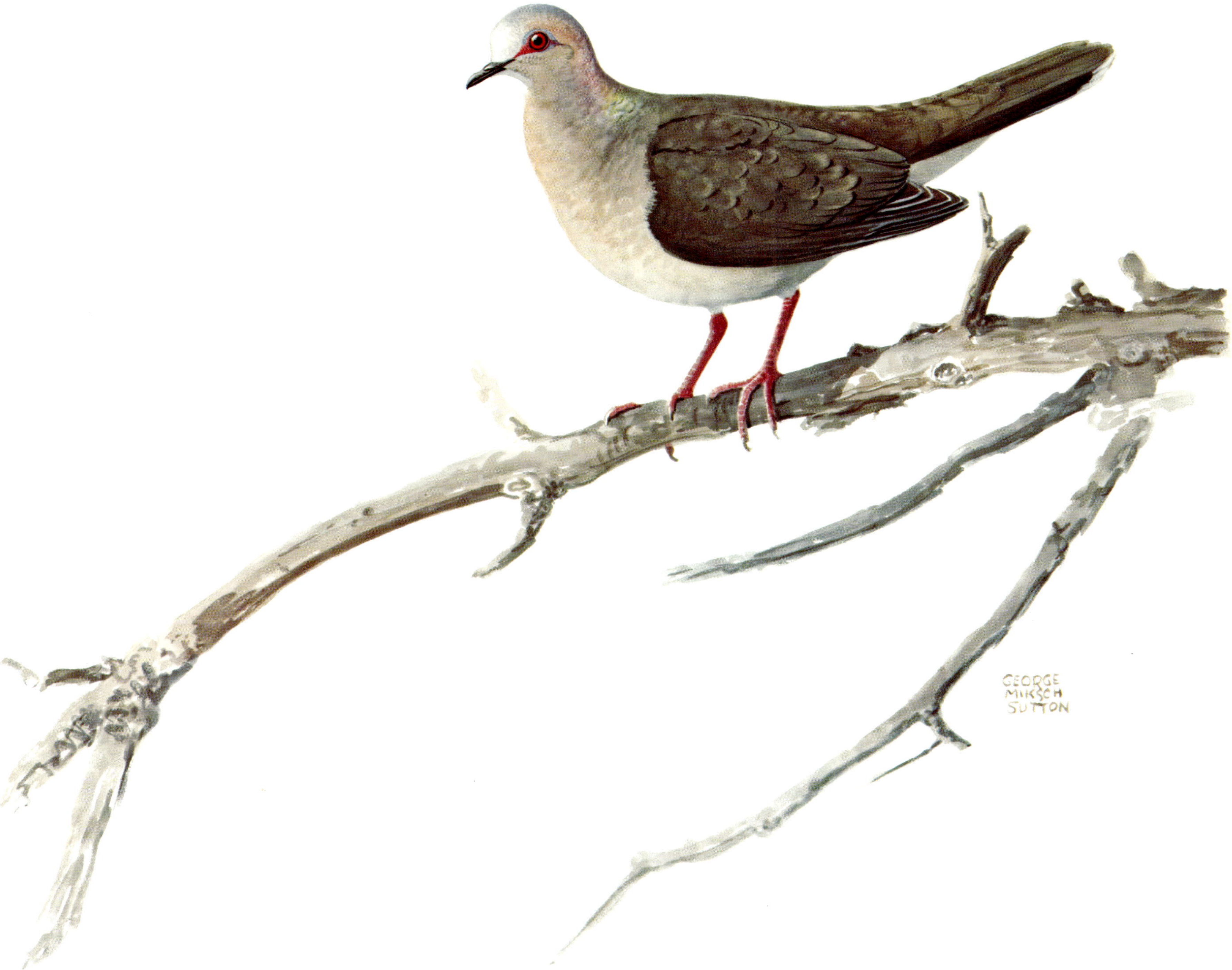
GEORGE
MIKSCH
SUTTON

MILITARY MACAW

The macaws are big, long-tailed New World parrots. The most northward ranging of them, and one of the dullest in color, is the Military Macaw (*Ara militaris*), a species found not only in Mexico, from Tamaulipas, Nuevo León, Chihuahua, and Sonora southward to Oaxaca, but also in South America (Venezuela to northern Argentina). The only other macaw found in Mexico, the Scarlet (*A. macao*), ranges widely southward through Central and South America to Bolivia and Brazil, but in Mexico is to be looked for only in Oaxaca, Chiapas, and southern Veracruz.

Macaws are called *guacomayos* by the Mexicans. In some areas the Military Macaw is hated because it does so much damage to the crops, especially corn. Perhaps because it is not brilliantly colored, it is not popular as a household pet, though it is frequently to be seen in zoos.

In 1938 (February 28 to March 5) and again in 1941 (March 12 to May 4), along the Río Sabinas in southwestern Tamaulipas, I was fortunate enough to see the Military Macaw almost every day. In 1938 the largest flock that we saw numbered eighty birds, in 1941, only sixty. The big birds were not by any means as plentiful as the much smaller parrots and parakeets, but we saw them fairly regularly mornings and evenings, and sometimes in the middle of the day. Their feeding grounds or roosting spots must have been somewhere upriver or down, for they did not often alight near the house or above the thatched huts just across the river. They all seemed to be paired. The small flocks invariably numbered from four to six or eight birds, never three to seven, and the big flocks were always of even number.

The small flocks that alighted near the house were easy enough to see if they were in a dead tree, but among leaves they were virtually invisible until they started to move. The flocks that stopped near us never seemed to be after food.

We often left the breakfast table to watch the macaws going over. If we heard that fearsome squawk we knew they would presently be overhead, for their line of flight almost always followed the river. Watching from below was rewarding, for the yellow of the underwings imparted a beauty that was not visible when the bird was perching.

The *guacomayos* were truly impressive. Their wings moved slowly, majestically. As the flock flew over, one bird sometimes gave forth an ear-splitting squawk, but there was no shrill chatter like that of the parakeets, no rapid repetition of certain phrases like those that some of the parrots gave. When I went out to watch I did not return until the macaws had passed out of sight. I remembered, as I stood there, how the long freight trains of childhood had fascinated me. I never felt that the train was gone until the caboose was out of sight.

We were told that the *guacomayos* did not nest until after the rains in August. We saw no sign of nesting activity, and the reproductive organs of specimens obtained on March 27 and April 27 were not enlarged. At El Salto, the wonderful waterfall in San Luis Potosí, we guessed that the several pairs of Military Macaws that were flying about might be nesting in niches among the rocks.

Recent letters from the Sabinas Valley have saddened me, for they have reported that no one sees macaws there any more. To see them nowadays it is necessary to go west of the big foothills. This is hard to believe for one who saw them every day only thirty years ago—and harder still to bear.

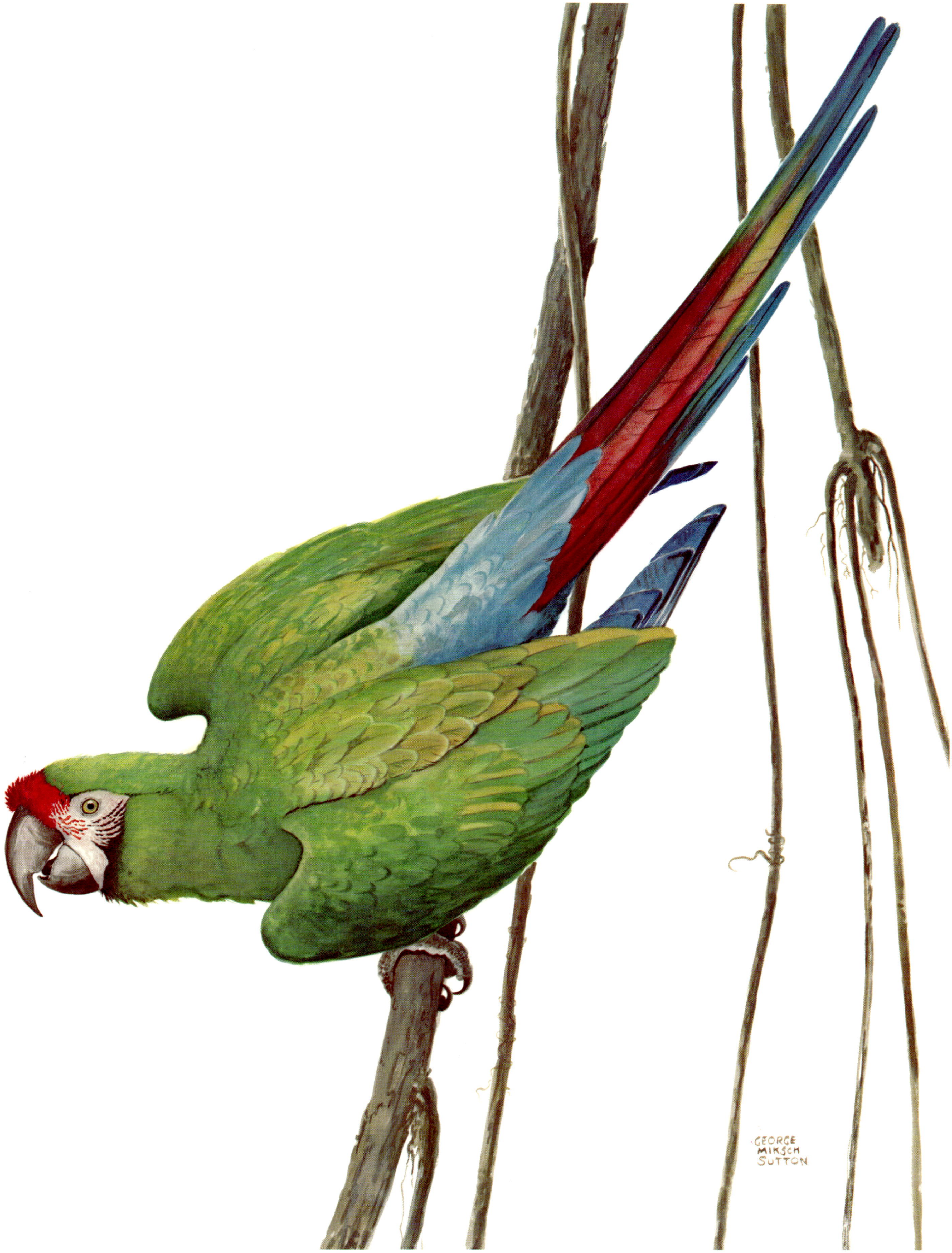
GEORGE
MIKSCH
SUTTON

GREEN PARAKEET

When John Semple, Tom Burleigh, and I first traveled to Mexico in 1938, we hoped to obtain at least one specimen of each species of bird that we saw—these "for the record." As we moved southward from Laredo we continued for quite a while to see not new and puzzling "exotic" birds, but the same hawks, shrikes, mockingbirds, and pyrrhuloxias that we had been seeing in Texas. The whole countryside looked a good deal like Texas, too. But at Monterrey we found a few birds that we had never seen before, among them the Rose-throated Becard (*Platypsaris aglaiae*) and Rufous-capped Warbler (*Basileuterus rufifrons*). Near Victoria we came upon truly tropical species, such as the Bare-throated Tiger Heron (*Tigrisoma mexicanum*) and Lineated Woodpecker (*Dryocopus lineatus*). And finally, near the village of Gómez Farías in southwestern Tamaulipas, in lush woodland that reached from the banks of the Río Sabinas up onto the first foothill of the Sierra Madre Oriental, we found ourselves in a new world. Here a familiar bird, a truly familiar one, was the exception. To see familiar species we had to leave the heavy woods and retrace our way eastward out onto the comparatively dry coastal plain.

About us in this verdant wonderland were parrots, parrots galore. They ranged in size from that of the little Aztec Parakeet (*Aratinga astec*), about 10 inches long, to that of the great Military Macaw (*Ara militaris*), whose fearful squawks made the spine tingle even when heard at a distance of half a mile. Hesitant to shoot any parrot, since we supposed that the Mexicans might make a little money selling them to dealers, we sheepishly inquired if it would be all right for us to obtain a specimen of each of the several species. The response was wholehearted, if not overwhelming: "Take them all!"

The fact was, of course, that the parrots ate what the Mexicans tried to raise in their little fields. The Aztec Parakeets and Green Parakeets (*Aratinga holochlora*) were so timid that the children could frighten them off with a bit of yelling and hand-slapping; but the middle-sized parrots, all of them short-tailed, would not leave until they saw the children picking up stones; and the sage macaws, knowing that the stones would be small and not very painful at worst, would reach down deliberately, tear off whole ears of corn, and fly majestically off with them.

Shrillest of all were the Green Parakeets, which often visited tall trees near our house at the Rancho Rinconada, eating fruit, buds, and flowers. I am not sure that they actually ate the petals, stamens, or pistils, but they surely tore the blossoms to pieces. When, frightened by a sudden sound, they flew out and away, the din of their screeching was beyond belief. Fortunately it did not last long, for the flock flew fast, and once they had departed they did not usually return until the following day.

Near the village of Xilitla (pronounced Heel-eat-la) in San Luis Potosí is a cave in which Green Parakeets were roosting at the time of our visit in late December, 1951. There Bob Newman, Charlie Shaw, Richard Graber, his wife Jean, and I watched the parakeets as they alighted on vines hanging down over the cave's mouth. While we were in the cave a Peregrine Falcon (*Falco peregrinus*) came by, put the shrieking flock of parakeets to flight, and carried off one of the birds. I could not help wondering whether the falcon paid the cave that sort of visit every afternoon.

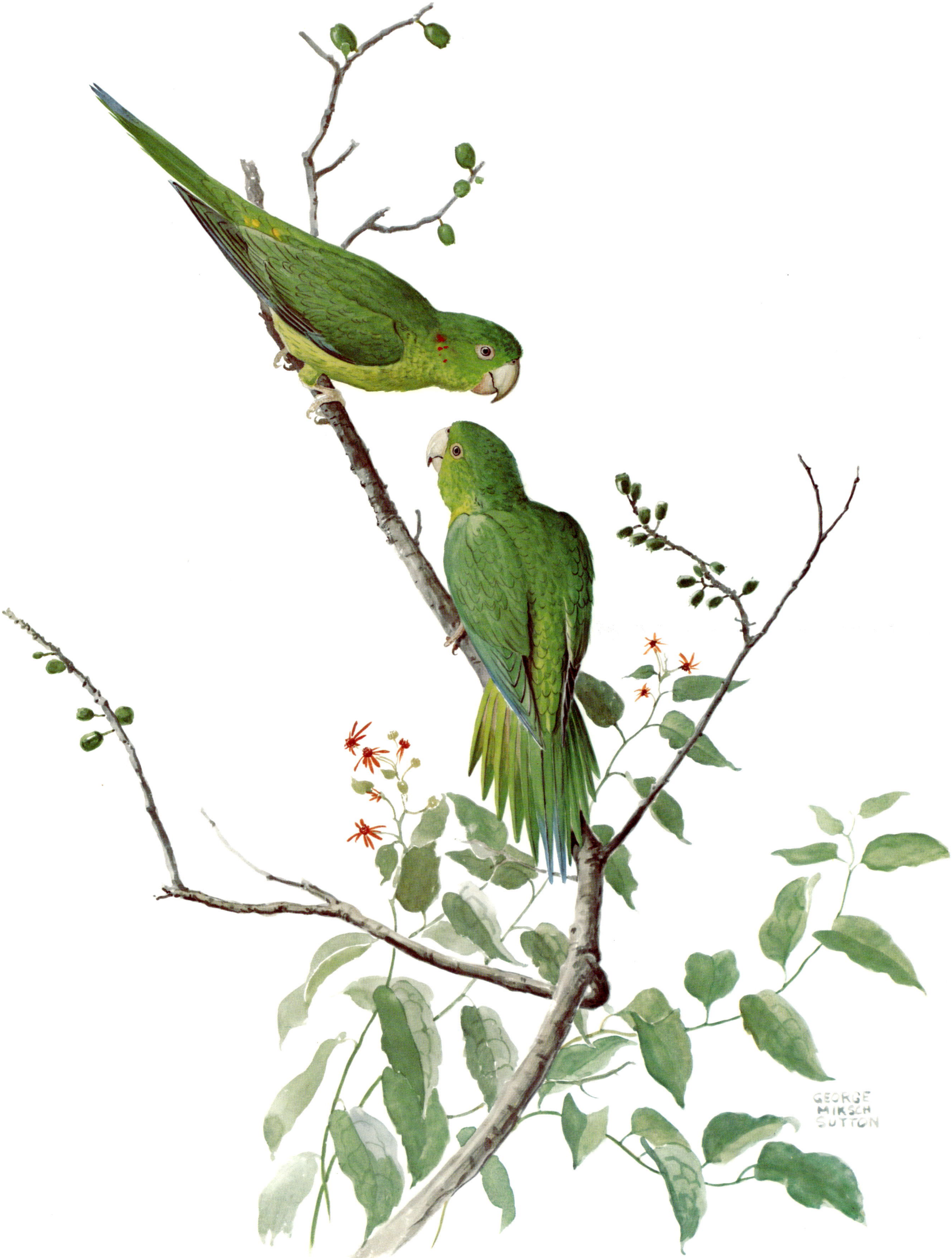
GEORGE
MIKSCH
SUTTON

YELLOW-HEADED PARROT

The Yellow-headed Parrot *(Amazona ochrocephala)* is a well-known cage bird. It can be bought in pet shops the world over. So often is it called "Polly," whether it be male or female, and so often asked if it wants a cracker, that it probably expects the worst when someone offers it a tidbit without saying something suitably inane.

For reasons now beyond me I called this parrot the "double yellowhead" as a boy. That word *double* may have puzzled me, but it never bothered me, for a great many bird names were strange. I accepted it along with the others. Not until I had had a chance to watch wild yellowheads along the north edge of their range in Mexico did I understand how such a name could have come into use. There, along the Río Corona, not far from the little village of Güemes, Tamaulipas, I watched the yellowheads feeding in tall trees directly above me. That day I saw one bird, suddenly excited, puzzled, or angered—I had no way of knowing which—lift every feather of its head in such a way as to appear almost comical. He was, indeed, double-headed, and he stayed that way for a full minute or more. Here is what I wrote in my book *Mexican Birds* concerning those wonderful hours with my first wild parrots:

"The parrots quieted down while feeding—an important fact that I did not know at first. Eventually I learned that the surest way of finding them at a meal was not through listening for their cries, nor yet by following them up and down the river, but by standing quietly beneath the ebony trees waiting for the falling of a bean pod. An odd, unreasonable sound that pop! on the dry leaves. No wind, apparently no disturbance in the treetop, yet down would fall the 5- or 6-inch-long seed container of the giant legume, ripped apart and dropped by an unseen yellowhead.

"I chanced to note a company of eight parrots flying quietly to a distant ebony. With the binocular I watched them climbing this way and that, each to a pod, as they set to work feeding. Presently I stalked them, approaching by a devious route so that they should not be able to see me. Not once did they chatter or screech. Not once did they flap or flutter. Being genuinely busy, they had no time for hilarity. Standing at last directly under them, I marveled at my inability to see them. Bright, even gaudy creatures that I knew them to be, they were invisible. Nor did I hear so much as the briefest call note. All that I heard was a low, steady, slightly breathy sound of munching, punctuated by sharp little clickings as pieces of pod hit leaves on their way to the ground.

"An odd accident befell me as I listened to the parrots breakfasting above me. A big, dry, neatly chambered pod, tough as a piece of coconut shell and astonishingly heavy, dropped straight onto my head. For an instant I wondered if Semple [one of my companions that day], who was perfectly capable of such untoward behavior, might be playing a trick on me. At length, coming to my senses, I placed the blame on myself, where it belonged. Had not an old Mexican proverb warned us that he who sneaks under breakfast tables may well expect a crumb in the eye or a kick in the face?"

My painting, made along another river several years later, shows a male bird after it has lifted its head plumage, thus becoming a "double yellowhead." As for the "old Mexican proverb" mentioned, it was one of several composed by me as occasion demanded.

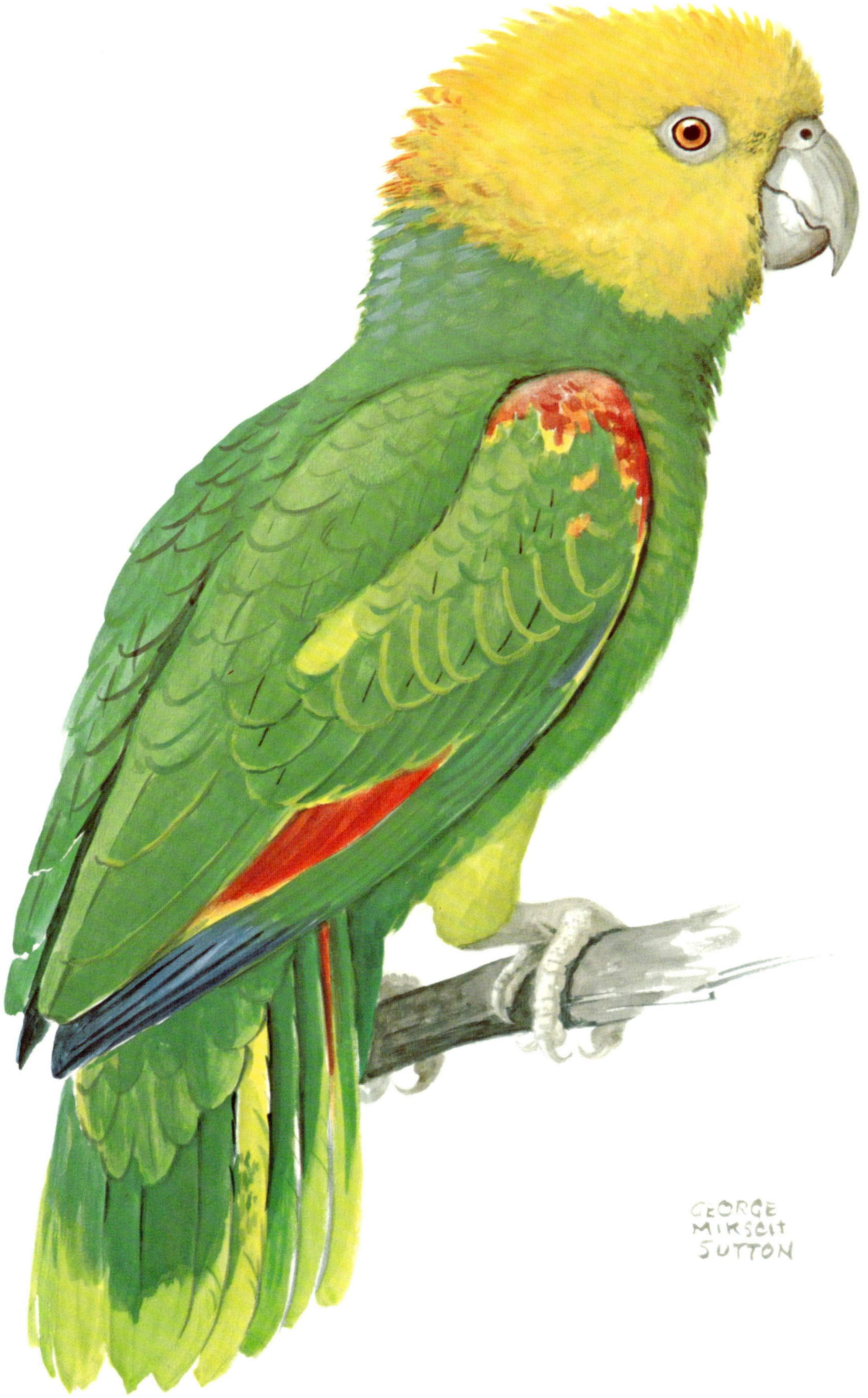
GEORGE
MIKSCH
SUTTON

RED-CROWNED PARROT

Whenever I visit northeastern Mexico I expect to see a good deal of the Red-crowned Parrot (*Amazona viridigenalis*). It is one of the "specialities" of the region, for it is found nowhere else in the world. It ranges over parts of Nuevo León, Tamaulipas, San Luis Potosí, and Veracruz. Whether it breeds throughout the area it occupies remains to be ascertained. So far as I know, it is strictly non-migratory, but it probably moves about, becoming commonplace when certain foods are abundant and withdrawing if there is a food shortage.

At the Rancho Rinconada in southwestern Tamaulipas in the spring of 1941 we came to consider the red-crown one of the commonest birds. Certainly it was among the noisiest. Its shrill, clearly enunciated *heelo, crack, crack, crack* was a familiar sound every morning while the birds were moving about feeding, and every evening when great flocks passed downriver, presumably to a communal roosting place. Usually they fed high in big trees. If we wanted a good look at them we hid ourselves along the river near a big clump of bamboo in which they often gathered not far above ground. We never learned precisely what they were eating there. They had an amusing way of climbing out a tough stalk, getting closer to the end, weighting it down until we wondered if it might snap, then, head down, hanging nonchalantly on with one foot while nibbling at something held in the other.

It would not surprise me to learn that red-crowns often mate for life. In mid-March most of the birds that we saw were paired. Even when the big flocks passed over we could see that the pairs were keeping together. We did observe sparring among rival males, however, and occasionally we watched two birds fighting in midair, facing each other and fluttering upward as if climbing an invisible wire. I enjoyed watching one bird as it walked a long way on a branch before presenting a tiny tidbit to another bird, probably its mate. When moving along a really big branch a red-crown used its beak almost constantly, sometimes grasping the bark, sometimes using the top of its upper mandible as a third foot.

On the last day of March, 1941, I observed two or three pairs of red-crowns quarreling over a nest-site—an old lineated woodpecker hole in a big cypress about 60 feet above the river's edge. One pair finally won out. From that time on, we usually saw single birds or small flocks rather than pairs along that stretch of river. Whenever we struck the base of the cypress or made a noise under the tree, out would pop the head of a red-crown. Even though the bird was a long way up, we could tell that it was "giving us the eye" as only an annoyed parrot can.

My painting was made at Paño Ayuctle along the Río Sabinas in late May, 1947. I was a guest of my friends Ernest P. Edwards and Robert B. Lea that year. I had a living bird as my model, not someone's pet, but a slightly crippled bird that I happened upon as it was trying to fly off with a flock that had gathered at the river's edge. Possibly it had struck a branch as it was flying down to the water's edge. Of course it squawked and bit savagely when caught, but it "tamed down" remarkably when talked to. It never quite forgave me; that was clear enough from the look on its face.

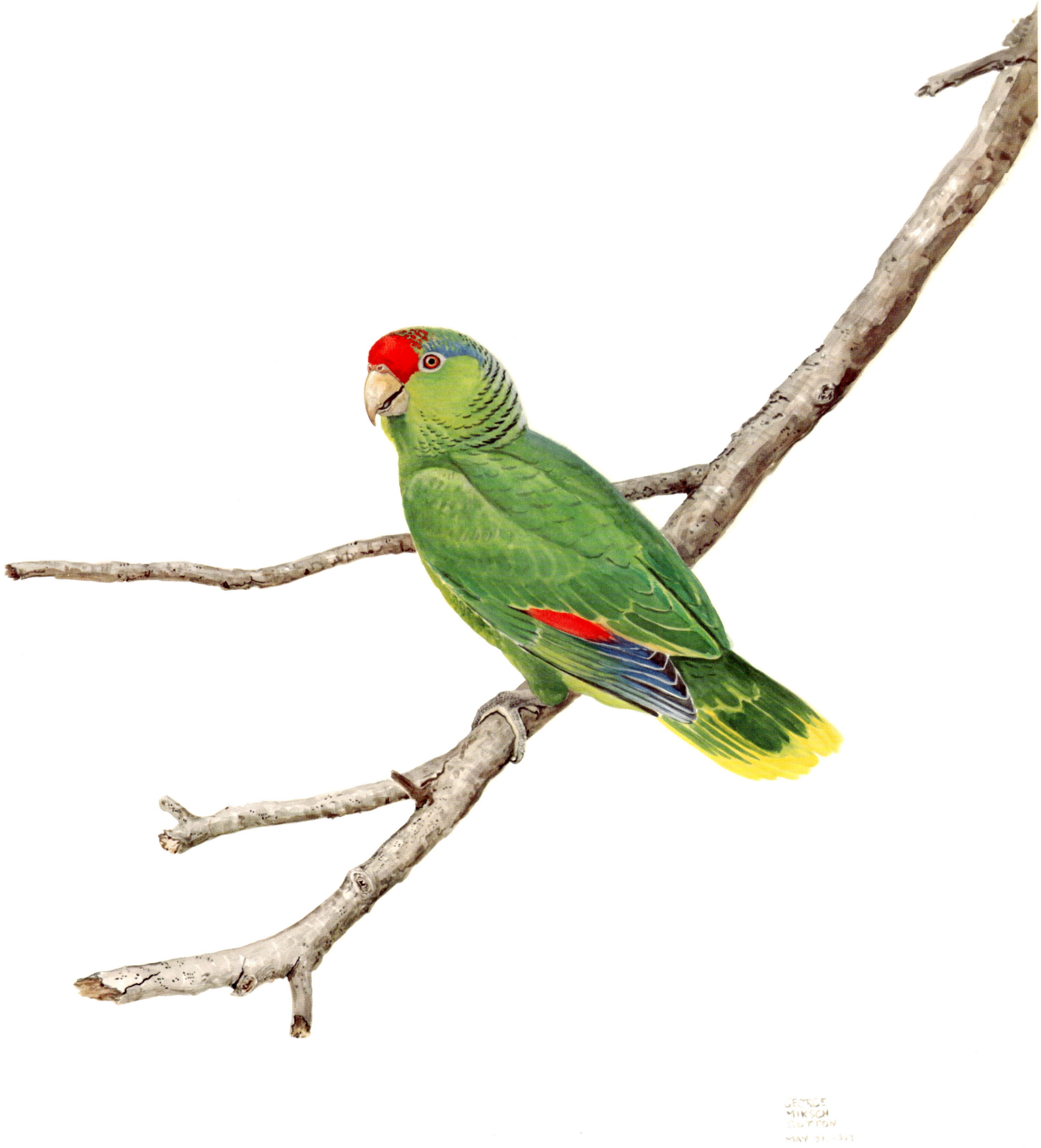
GEORGE
MIKSCH
SUTTON

MANGROVE CUCKOO

It was in the Everglades of Florida, fifty years ago, that I saw my first Mangrove Cuckoo *(Coccyzus minor)*. There the species deserved its name because it actually lived among the mangroves and, so far as I could see, nowhere else. I had a hard time finding it, for work among those strange trees-on-stilts involved clambering over and around the tangled roots and wading in water and mud of varying depth, not to mention the cruel saw-grass, the mosquitoes, which were disagreeable though not numerous, and the alligators, one of which I almost stepped on. The alligator, about 6 feet long, was probably asleep. I may actually have touched it with my foot. At any rate, it was badly frightened, so it thrashed the water with its tail as it rushed off, showering me with mud from head to foot. The cuckoo, when finally I found it, was not very wary, nor was it a particularly fine specimen, for it was molting. When I returned to "civilization" I probably embellished the alligator episode, describing in detail the open mouth, snapping jaws, etc. of "the monster." I did not want to disappoint those who were listening. Appropriately enough, the lake where I had obtained the cuckoo specimen was known as "Gator Lake."

In Mexico *Coccyzus minor* is said to inhabit the mangroves of both coasts from Tamaulipas in the east and Sinaloa in the west southward, but I think of it as a bird not of coastal vegetation but of semi-arid brush well inland, for that is where I found it in 1947— first along the Río Sabinas not far from the town of El Limón (May 17 to 27), then on the very top of the Mesa de Llera, not far south of Victoria, on June 2. The fact that our various parties did not record the species in any way during earlier visits to northeastern Mexico (1938, 1939, 1941) continues to puzzle me. We saw and heard the bird fairly often in 1947. Its call, a strange, rather deliberate *kah, kah, kah, goo, goo, goo*, was a familiar sound along the river itself and in the thicketty woods east of camp, out on the coastal plain, but not in the heavy woods on the foothill west of the river. Those fine foothill trees, refreshed as they were by daily showers and sheltered from the sun by a cloud-banner, were truly tropical. Kinkajous, potoos, ocelots, and even jaguars lived in them.

I painted my picture on May 19. I remember the experience well. Having seen one of the cuckoos in an avocado tree near camp, I decided to show the bird perching on a fruit-bearing branch of that tree. While drawing the branch "direct from life," i.e., without cutting it off, I sat on a crudely slapped-together stool. Hard at work, absorbed in getting detail right, I happened to see a big tick crawling across the Fuertes paint-box, then another on the handle of one of the brushes, then—considerably to my annoyance—a whole army of them moving resolutely up the stool *and my pants*. Needless to say, it did not take me long to "get out of there." Abandoning the stool, removing the pants, shaking them fiercely, and pulling off such ticks as I could find on my legs, all helped. With lopped-off branch and unskinned bird on a table placed on ground that had long since been swept free of leaf-mold, I finished the drawing.

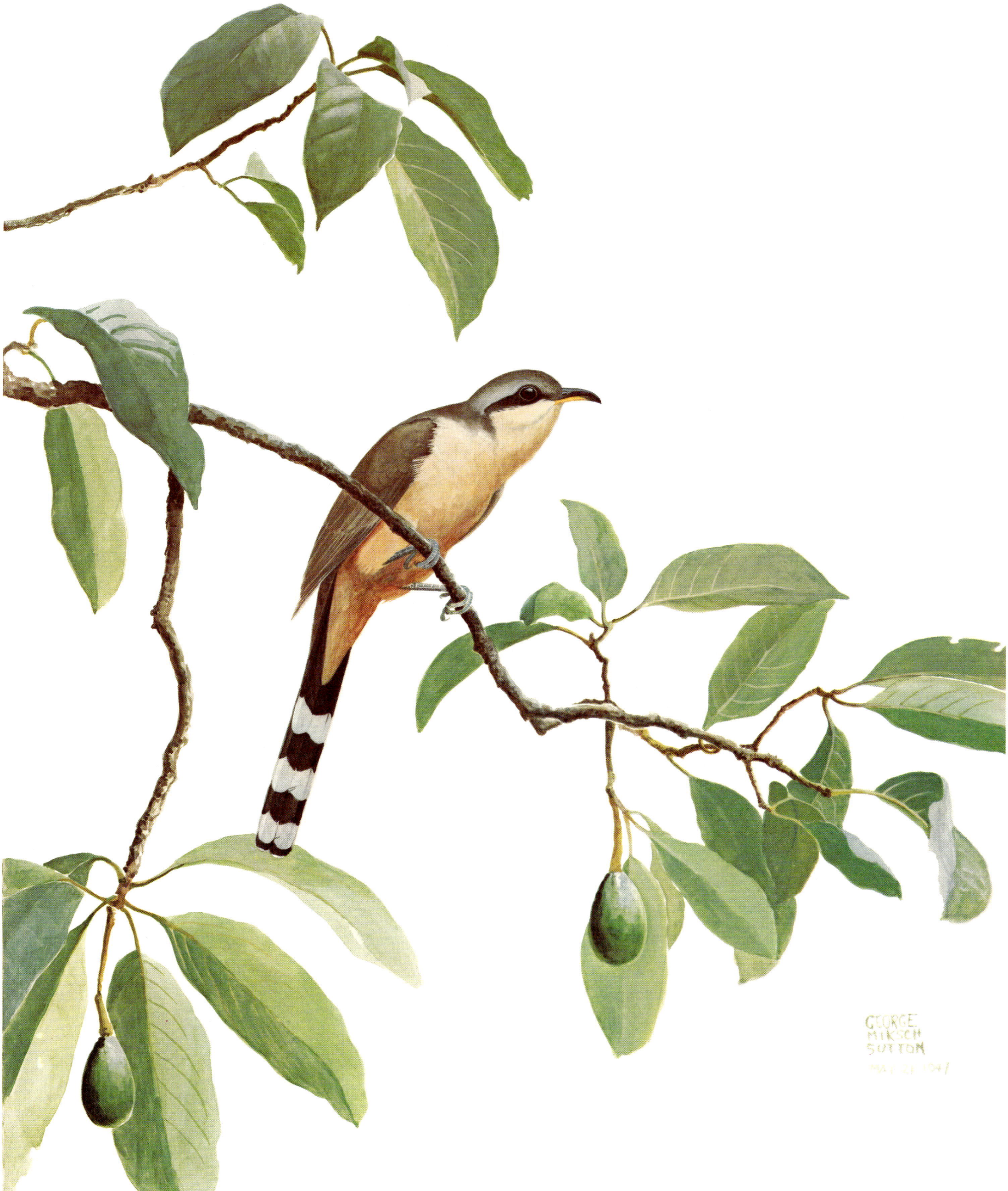
GEORGE
MIKSCH
SUTTON

SQUIRREL CUCKOO

The Squirrel Cuckoo *(Piaya cayana)*, so named because it looks like a reddish-brown squirrel, is found from northern Mexico (southern Sonora, southern Chihuahua, southern Tamaulipas) southward through Central America and South America as far as Peru and northern Argentina. In many parts of Mexico I have found it fairly common in open, mixed woodland up to elevations of about 5,000 feet. I have never seen it in forest like that through which the trail leads from Sabinal to Osmalón, San Luis Potosí. It is a slender bird, reddish brown on the whole head and upperparts, pale gray on the belly, with long tail of ten broad feathers, the outer pairs of which are largely black with bold white tips. The red-brown of the back and white tips of the tail feathers show plainly in flight, but *in* a tree the bird is often inconspicuous. This is partly because it has a habit of remaining motionless, except for a slow turning of the head, then slipping quickly to another perch, where it "freezes" again. Often it hops from perch to perch upward in a tree without opening its wings, then launches out from the top, gliding down into the next tree. Never have I seen it making a long flight from one high tree to another or from a point high on a hill downward into the valley. The fine red of its eyes does not show unless it pauses in full sunlight, but its pale green bill is noticeable.

The bird's calls, as I heard them in southern Tamaulipas, included a loud *keep-rear*, a sharp *kweep* repeated slowly several times, a low *kuck*, and an almost shrill *kee-ker*. My field-notes say nothing about a three-syllabled call such as the *hic-a-ro* heard in Costa Rica by my friend Alexander Skutch (1966, *Wilson Bulletin*, 78: 141). Birds that I have watched as they called held their heads high and opened their bills very wide, at the same time lifting their head feathers into a rough crest.

I saw my first Squirrel Cuckoo on February 27, 1938, shortly after our party arrived at the Rancho Rinconada in southwestern Tamaulipas. On my very first walk there, at a place where the trail forked, I hid myself and listened. A branch 15 feet above me suddenly shook, a leaf fell, and out into plain sight slipped an 18-inch-long slender bird. I saw at once that its whole head was brown, but that the color was paler below than above, and that the gray of the belly became darker, almost black, toward the tail. As the big cuckoo fell easily into flight, it spread its fine tail wide. It alighted in a thinly-leafed monkey's ear tree, giving me a brief look at its red eye and pale green bill. As it moved the long way of a branch it both hopped and ran.

Never have I visited the Río Sabinas without seeing the Squirrel Cuckoo, but I have not found its nest. Skutch tells us that in Costa Rica the nest is a "shallowly concave platform" with foundation of "long, coarse, straight, inflexible twigs, and lining of whole leaves"; the eggs, usually two, are "pure white, with a somewhat rough and chalky surface" (Skutch, *ibid.*, 146).

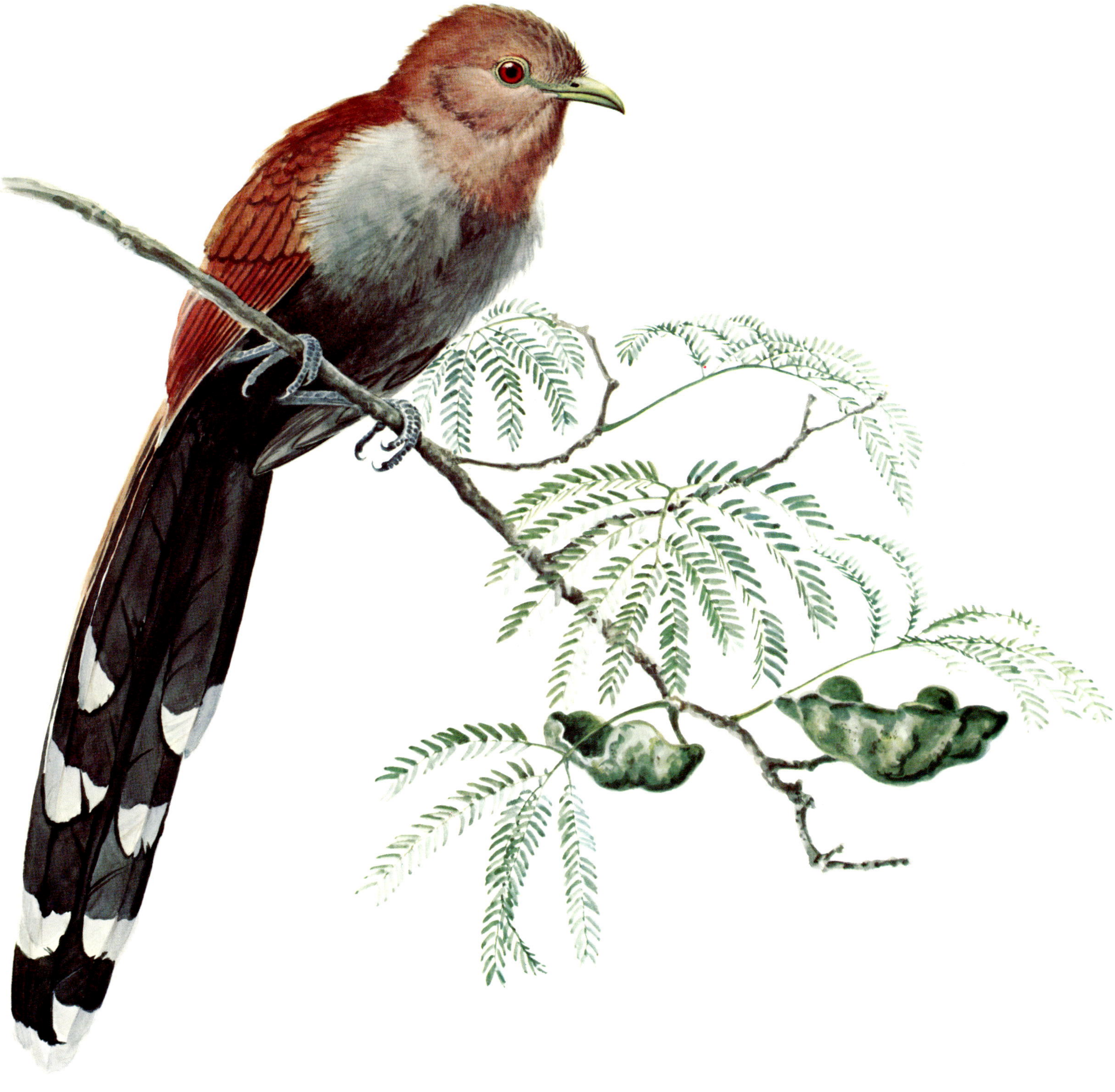

GROOVE-BILLED ANI

A familiar feature of Mexican lowlands is the tickbird or Groove-billed Ani *(Crotophaga sulcirostris)*, a loose-hung, not at all elegant member of the cuckoo family about a foot long and black all over, including bill, feet, eyelids, eyelashes, and eyes. The edges of some of its feathers are faintly iridescent, but the subtle bronzes, greens, and blues do not show much, even when struck directly by the sun. The bill is extraordinarily high and thin—a vagary of evolution beyond explanation. The tail has only eight feathers, another puzzling departure, for most cuckoos aside from the three anis of the genus *Crotophaga* have ten tail feathers.

The tickbird is slightly "spooky." This is not a scientific statement, of course, but what else is the proper adjective for creatures that go about in loose flocks uttering cries that sound more like gossip than defense of territory or declaration of joy, and that perch solemnly in shady undergrowth as if in silent conclave, each with back humped and tail hanging straight down, looking like a black cutout against the sunlit space beyond? One of the flock starts hopping sluggishly downward. Another does the same. Presently all are on the ground, moving through the brush like dark shadows, intent on following a line of ants. Whether eating the insects or stealing what the insects are carrying, they stay at the edge of the ant stream for a full hour, not uttering a sound, not bickering with each other over choice positions, and constantly on the move, eating, eating, eating, almost as if each item swallowed provided only energy enough for obtaining the next, and no more. Approach a flock of this sort slowly and the birds hop and climb into the bushes as if for conference, then flop down again, intent on finishing their meal. Approach one step more and off they all go, one or more of them giving an ill-defined, not at all noticeable cry that resembles the syllables *tick-cooly*, a transliteration that would never have occurred to me had not a young Mexican in Sinaloa told me that the local name for the bird was—as he wrote it—*ticuli*.

As I jotted this bit of information down I recalled that in Colima my friend Angel Lara had told me that everyone he knew called the bird the *ticús* (pronounced *tickoose*); that eating a *ticús* was bad; that whosoever ate a *ticús* might become sluggish, "dopey," even sexually impotent. Smiling impishly, he went on to say that if a woman knew her husband to be unfaithful she cooked a *ticús* and fed it to him, thereby reducing his amorousness to the point of making him *enticusado*. "You will not find that word in the dictionary," explained Angel, "but it's a good word. Everybody knows what it means."

To learn what an ani is like, follow one bird and watch closely. It manages to alight in the top of a bush despite the wind that, having almost toppled it, blows its tail first upward then so far to one side that the long axis of the tail is almost at right angles to that of the body. The bird sees a big wingless grasshopper on the ground. Down it goes, wings half spread. The tall grass hides it completely. Approach rapidly now, keeping low. There sits your bird, about 6 feet away, gulping grasshopper and inspecting you darkly through the waving blades. Did I use the word *spooky*? That is precisely what I meant.

My drawing was made at the Rancho del Cielo in southwestern Tamaulipas in the spring of 1941. In that part of Mexico the bird was called the *garrapatero*—meaning, quite literally, one who deals with (=eats) ticks. The vine with yellow flowers is of the well known genus *Bignonia*.

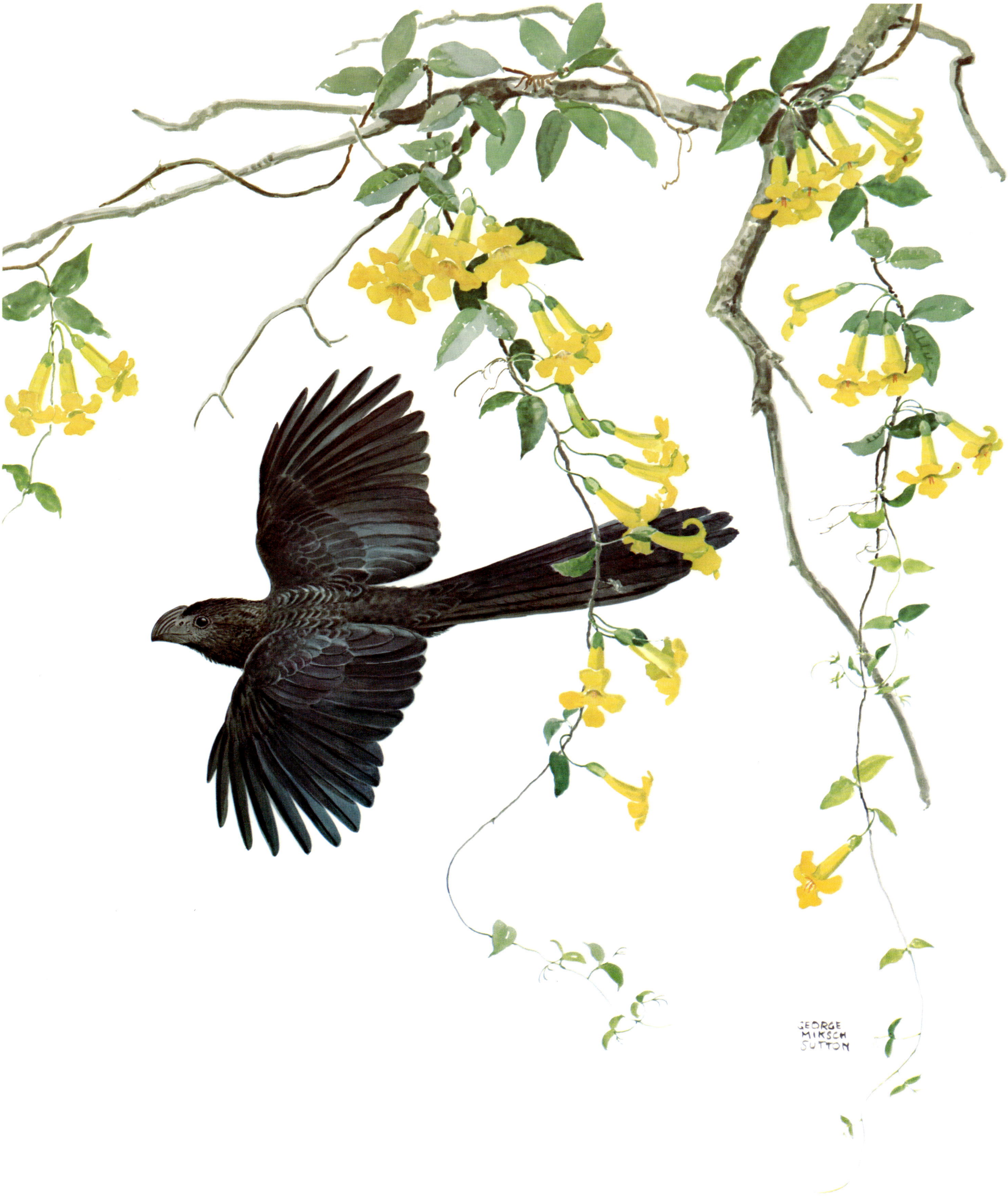
GEORGE
MIKSCH
SUTTON

NORTHERN PYGMY OWL

At the north end of Lake Pátzcuaro, about 11 kilometers west of the village of Quiroga, there is a wooded ravine that is made to order for the bird student. I first visited the delightful spot for an hour or so on February 3, 1949. From the dry streambed I could see big oaks and pines on the slopes above me. The woods were alive with birds, among them several species that would presently be leaving for their breeding grounds in the north. Below me, several kilometers off, stretched the shining expanse of Lake Pátzcuaro.

Three weeks later Roger Hurd and I returned to our ravine. Two ravens, circling overhead, croaked a welcome. During our four-day stay the weather was perfect—cool by night, pleasantly warm by day—though I couldn't help watching the sky, for I knew that a sudden cloudburst could wash us away, truck and all. I made two drawings there, one of hummingbirds bickering over flowers, the other of a Northern Pygmy Owl *(Glaucidium gnoma)*.

I'd never have made the latter had I not chanced to see one of the little owls alight in a madroño tree about 20 yards upslope from our truck while we were eating breakfast that first morning. The owl's perch was no hideout. When, an hour later, I saw the owl fly off, I felt sure that it had been sunbathing. Thinking back, I realized that it had flown in just as the bright rays had reached the ravine's bottom.

Taking cushions, drawing board, and paper to a comfortable spot about 20 feet from the madroño tree, I sketched in branch and leaves with pencil, hopeful that the owl would come back on the morrow. With picture thus laid out, I returned to the truck, thumbtacked another piece of paper to the drawing board, and went after hummingbirds.

The following morning I was at my madroño spot early. When the sun appeared, in flew the owl, right on schedule. At first suspicious, it glared at me and flicked its tail, then settled down, for that great brightness from the eastern sky was blissfully warm. This time I drew the owl, paying special attention to the bold markings on its underparts.

When I started to add paint, the madroño proved to be more troublesome than the owl, for the gloss on the big leaves was tricky. As the sun climbed, the highlights and deep shadows shifted perceptibly, convincing me at ten o'clock that what I'd done an hour earlier was all wrong. The owl's departure settled procedure. I would suspend owl-madroño operations and go after hummingbirds.

Early the third morning I was at my spot near the madroño. At sunup the owl appeared. For an hour I worked at highlights and shadows. By this time the owl regarded me and my paraphernalia as part of its habitat. Sunbath over, it flew off, thus telling me that hummingbird time had arrived. I finished the drawing, owl and all, on the fourth morning.

The Northern Pygmy Owl ranges from southeastern Alaska and northern British Columbia southward in the mountains to Guatemala. I had first seen the species in the spring of 1934 at the edge of the Forbidden Plateau on Vancouver Island, where it was one of the few birds inhabiting the climax coniferous forest. In Mexico I had found it at several localities, all of them well above sea-level. It was much like the Ferruginous Pygmy Owl *(G. brasilianum)* of the low country, and like that species came in two color phases, a reddish brown and a grayish brown. My bird of the ravine was of the reddish brown phase.

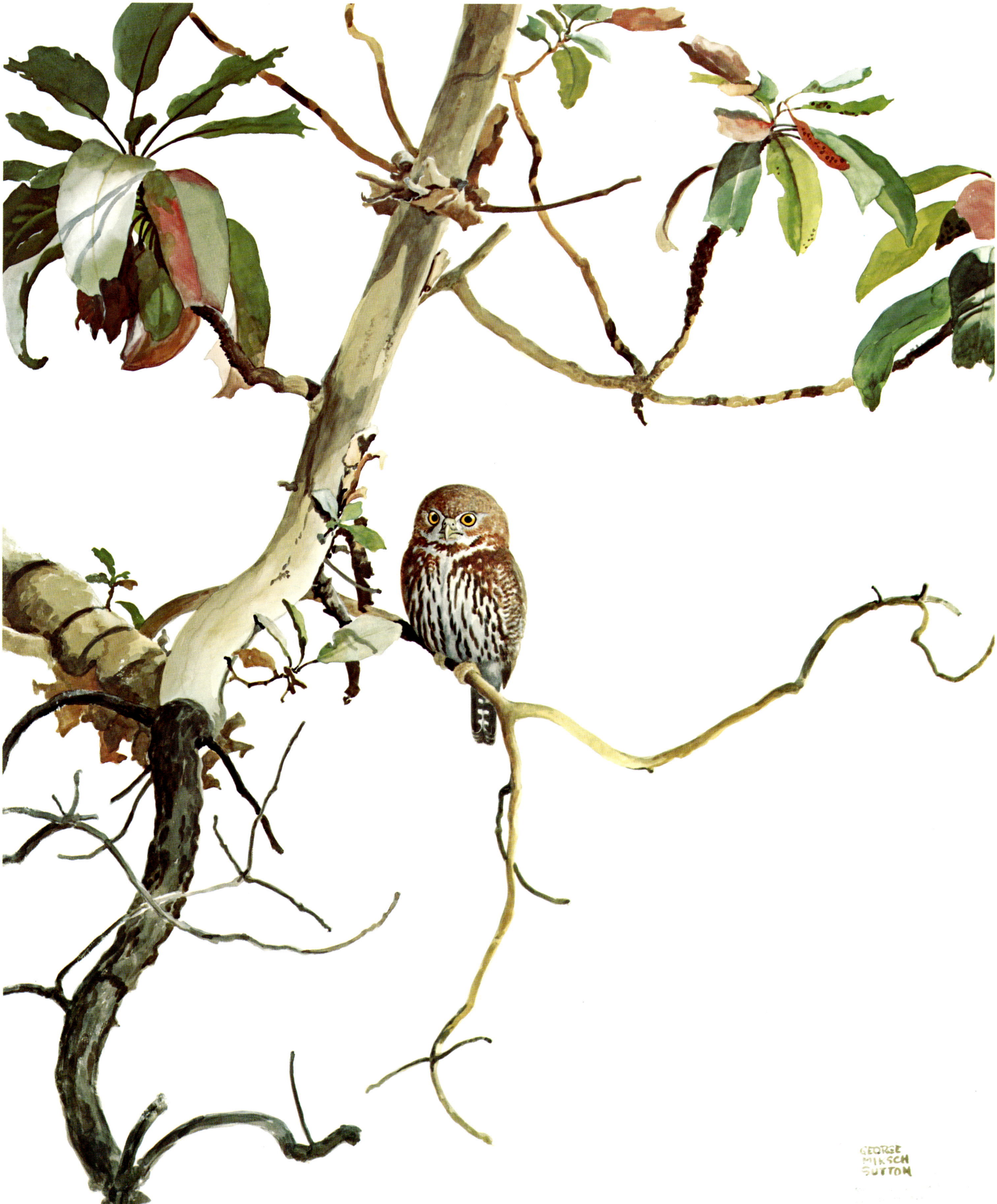
GEORGE
MIKSCH
SUTTON

FERRUGINOUS PYGMY OWL

An almost funny little owl that the Mexicans have nicknamed *"Cuatro Ojos"* (Four Eyes), because two dark spots on the back of the head look like eyes, is the Ferruginous Pygmy Owl *(Glaucidium brasilianum)*, a species found in low country from parts of the United States close to the Mexican border southward to southernmost South America. Like many owls, it is more often heard than seen, though it is by no means exclusively nocturnal. Its somewhat monotonous call, a rapidly repeated *poot, poot, poot, poot*, continued indefinitely at a rate of two or three *poots* per second, reminds me of the exhaust from a little engine. Along the Río Moctezuma at Tamazunchale, San Luis Potosí, in April of 1939, I heard this call every day at a certain spot and looked for the owl over and over, without once seeing it. At the Hacienda el Cóbano, near the fine city of Colima, I heard the call every morning in January, 1971, yet never saw the bird until, much later in the day, Mary P. Williams, one of the ladies attending an ornithological seminar, showed it to me on a high branch long after it had stopped calling. How she happened to see it I shall never know. There it sat, in perfectly plain sight and perfectly still, taking a sunbath.

Along the Río Sabinas in southwestern Tamaulipas we often heard and saw the little owl. One day while returning to the house from the river I heard the fierce squeaking of a hummingbird, not from flowers along the path or from a tree above me, but from a palmetto thicket. Knowing that the squeaks were a battle-cry, I investigated. What I saw first was, of course, the hummer, perched on a dead weed about 4 feet up. The tiny bird turned its head and jerked its body from side to side as it squeaked, then suddenly darted toward the base of a palmetto, backed up, darted in again—toward what looked like a brown knob not a great deal larger than a hummer—on the stem of one of the lowest of the palmetto's great fans. The knob shrank each time the hummer attacked. Presently I saw that the knob had golden yellow eyes. As these opened wide, I began to comprehend the feelings of the hummer.

Later that day (March 3, 1938), drawn by the alarm cries of a tanager high in a cypress at the river's edge, I saw another Ferruginous Pygmy Owl near the end of a long branch. Since we needed a specimen, I shot it. It fell into a deep part of the river, too far out to be reached with a long stick. Floating high, the specimen started slowly downstream, then, to my intense annoyance, it disappeared for a second. A fish had grabbed it. When it went under a second time, I shot—this time to drive away the fish—hurried to the river's edge, yanked off my clothes, and swam for the owl. So excited was I during all this that I was not conscious of one important fact until I started putting on my clothes: I had undressed in the middle of a flourishing thicket of poison ivy.

The stomach of the specimen contained (among other items) a large, strangely shaped "stink bug" that had been swallowed whole. I decided to show this insect in my drawing, so placed it in the foot of one of the owls. I think that what I have shown is accurate, though photographs taken at owls' nests at night have shown the parent owls carrying food in their beaks.

Two Ferruginous Pygmy Owl nests that we found in San Luis Potosí in 1939 were in old woodpecker holes. One, near Tamazunchale, that held two eggs on April 27 was about 12 feet up; the other, near the village of El Xolol, was 15 feet up and held three eggs on April 29.

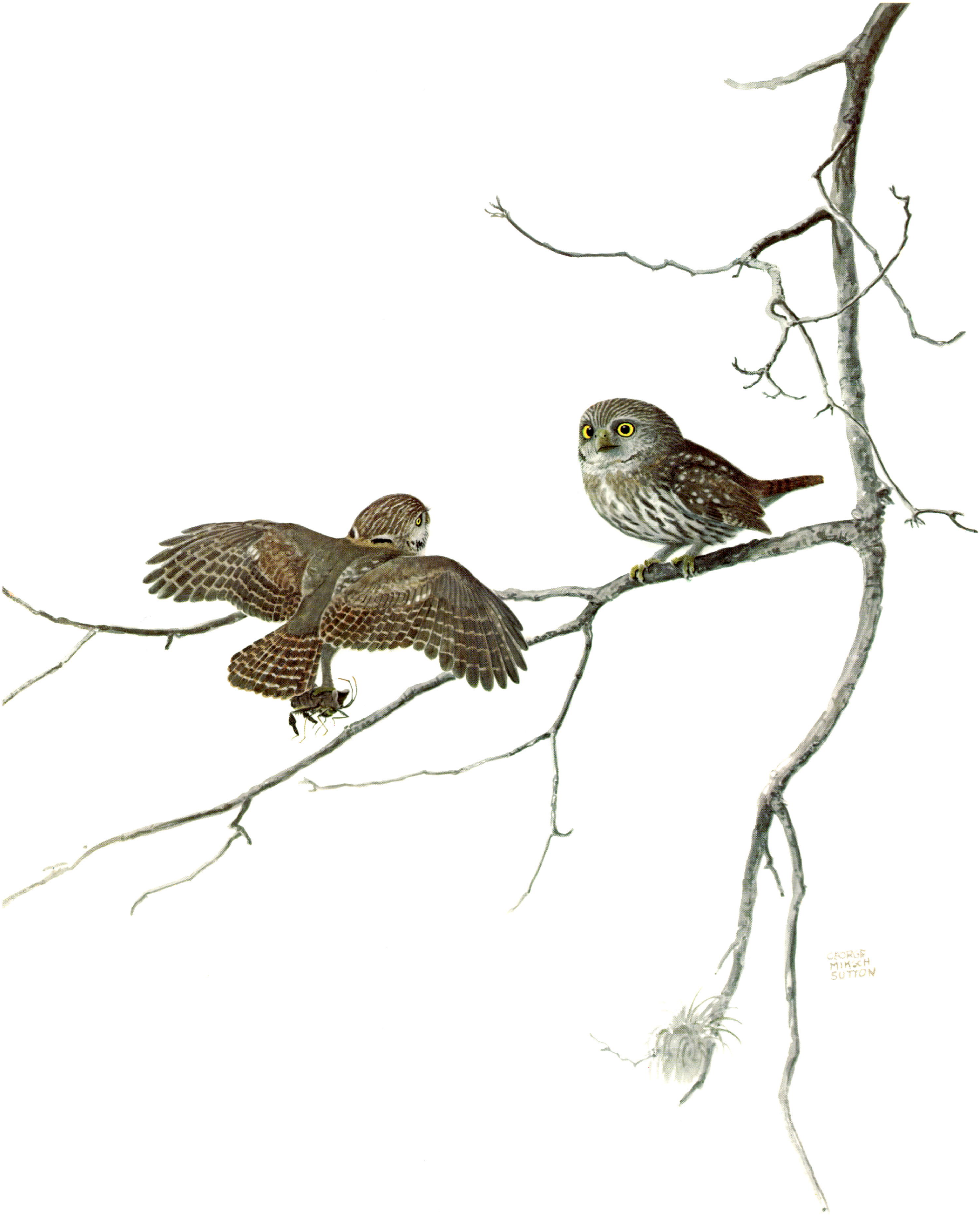
GEORGE
MIKSCH
SUTTON

GREEN-BREASTED MANGO

Among the handsomest of Mexico's hummingbirds is the Green-breasted (or Prevost's) Mango *(Anthracothorax prevostii)*, a rather large hummingbird that I have seen much of along the north edge of its range. I believe it is migratory. Along the Río Sabinas in southwestern Tamaulipas, where it is common in summer, we did not see it between March 12 and the end of that month in 1941, but during the first three days of April we saw males repeatedly, on April 4 we collected a female, and on April 5 we observed a female gathering nest material. Pairing must have been accomplished very promptly that season; or perhaps the birds had paired while in their winter quarters or on their way northward.

Since many of the flowers that the Green-breasted Mangos visited were low, we often saw the birds at eye-level. Several males at the Rancho Rinconada had favorite perches six to 15 feet above ground in brushy woods well back from the river. They were contentious, as hummers usually are. As they moved from one perch or feeding spot to another they bounded along, chippering like little swifts, their wings a blur except at the very top of a bound when for a split second they were sometimes perceptible, each sticking straight out horizontally from the body. The females seemed to stay close to the river. Rarely did we see them in the thicket near the house, and I don't recall ever seeing one female chasing another.

On April 10 I watched a female gathering cobwebs and followed her to her nest. To my surprise, the half-finished structure was at least 50 feet up near the end of a long branch in a towering cypress at the river's edge. Once discovered, it was fairly conspicuous, though I could not see much detail from the ground, even with the binocular. Believing that my friend Sewall Pettingill would want to obtain photographs of the bird at work, I showed him the nest. His comment was scornful: "Man alive, what do you take this camera for? That nest's a mile high!" Thus disposed of, I decided that the problems of a bird artist weren't so bad after all.

I continued to include that high nest in my regular rounds. On April 12 the tiny structure appeared to be finished, but the female was in it, moving her head now this way, now that, binding it all together with spider webbing.

On April 18 she was sitting deep in the nest, her bill, tail, and wingtips sticking out over the edge. As she flew off a short way and returned, her wingbeats seemed to be slower than those of the males I had been watching. I last visited the nest on April 29, almost three weeks after I had found it. There the faithful female was, as usual. I could not help wondering what was under her. Egg-laying had required at least two days, incubation at least fourteen days. How I longed to see the young ones about the time they took their first flight!

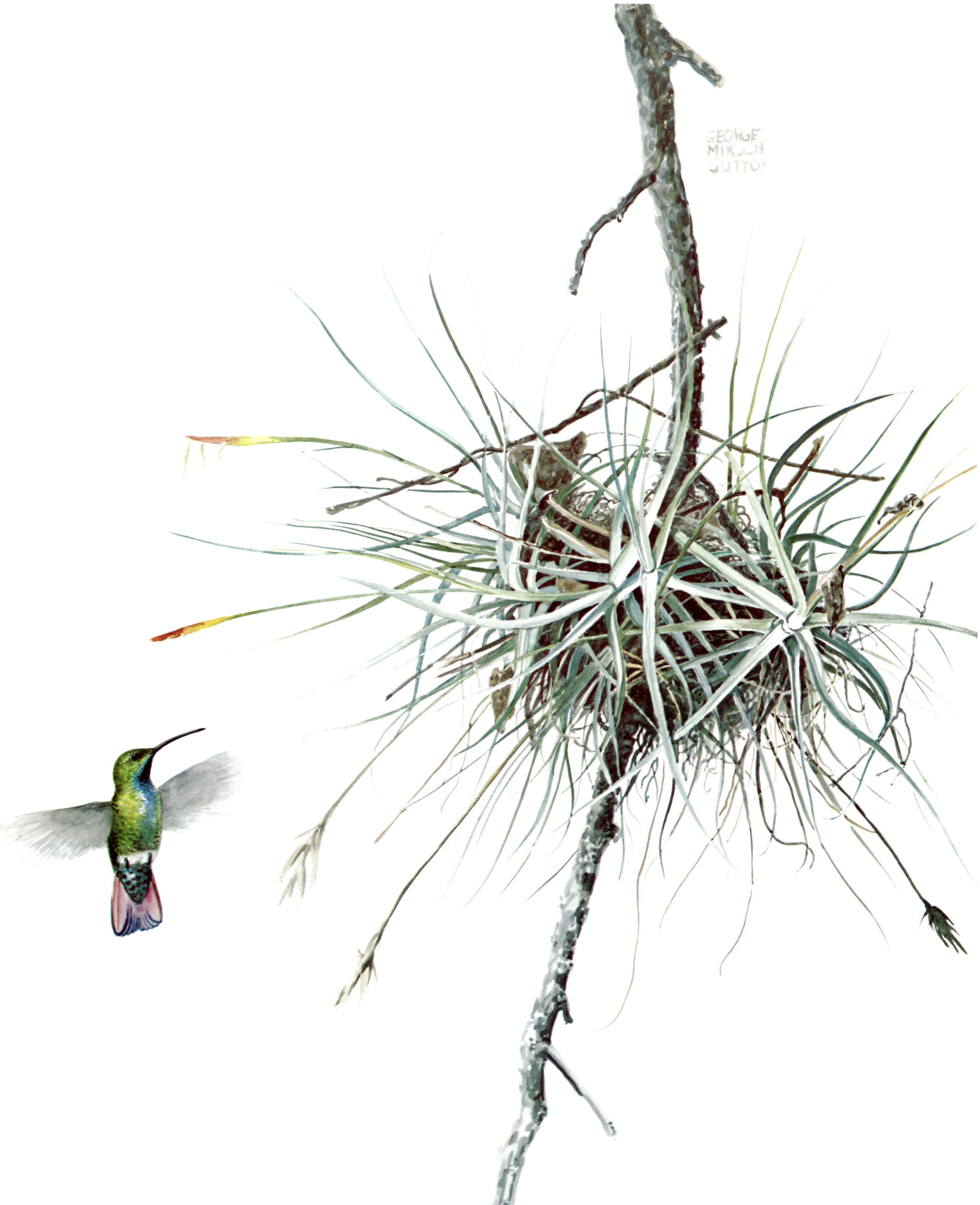
GEORGE
MIKSCH
SUTTON

WHITE-EARED HUMMINGBIRD

Among the liveliest of Mexico's birds is the *Chupaflor Orejiblanco*, the flowersucker with white ear, the bird the books call the White-eared Hummingbird *(Hylocharis leucotis)*. The species ranges northward across the United States border into southernmost Arizona, where it has not yet been found nesting, and southward to El Salvador and Nicaragua. A mountain dweller, it is remarkably hardy, a fact I was to learn firsthand at about 10,000 feet elevation in Michoacán where I saw a nest with two fresh eggs on February 19, 1949. The nest was about 3 feet up in a shrub on the edge of a grassy field. The night before had been genuinely cold. Heavy frost had covered the grass earlier that morning. At a lower elevation (about 8,500 feet) during the preceding two weeks I had seen two nests, one holding two well-developed young on February 8, the other, two young a bit smaller than bumblebees on February 10. At that camp the noisy chipping of White-eared Hummingbirds was almost incessant during the warm daylight hours. The chips were often given in groups of four: *chi-chi-chi-chip*. The sound was not part of the early morning bird chorus. At that chilly hour the White-ears were still quiescent, waiting for the climbing sun to speed up the rate of their basal metabolism enough to set their wings to beating. Just before noon on February 6, at this same camp, a loud chipping overhead attracted my attention to a White-ear describing arcs above the trees—probably a courtship display of some sort.

I became intimately acquainted with the White-ear at our camp 11 kilometers west of Quiroga, Michoacán, at the north end of Lake Pátzcuaro. There several of the tiny birds regularly visited festive clumps of flowering lobelia at the edge of a dry streambed. Wanting to make my drawing authentic, I searched for a spot at which I could sit comfortably in the shade while drawing flowers and birds direct from life. The spot I chose was the thick root of a tree not very far from our truck.

The hummingbirds were bold enough as I carried drawing board and paints to my seat, and once I had ensconced myself they became even bolder. Often they fed within a foot or so of my face, though I doubt that I could have moved my hand fast enough to have caught one. So heedless of me were they that two of them often tangled right in front of me, the iridescent greens and blues of their plumage and the red of their bills flashing brightly. At times a feeding bird was so close that I could see pollen gathering on its head from stamens that stuck out well beyond the tips of the petals. This was the plant's way of making the hummingbirds work for them.

The lobelia itself interested me considerably, for its manner of growth varied from place to place. In open fields it was a neat, usually small bush; but in the shade near our camp it was almost a vine. I looked in vain for evidence that the plants away from the shade had been eaten back by livestock. Could the fact that sunlight surrounded them there have determined their over-all shape?

GEORGE
MIKSCH
SUTTON

GREEN VIOLET-EAR

The hummingbirds—the some 300 species of the family taken as a whole—are a kind of eighth wonder of the world. Their colors, flashing with heliographic brilliancy, dazzle the eye. Their beholder learns from the physicist that those bright colors are "structural," that they are only partly, if at all, pigmentary, that they are a kind of illusion resulting from the absorption of parts of the light rays that pass through the feathers and a rejection or throwing back of the parts that are not absorbed.

A bit stunned by the esoteric language, and still incredulous, the beholder looks again. The throat of the specimen in his hand is a resplendent green, the top of the head an equally resplendent purple. *The very shape of the minute interlocking strands that go to make up those tiny feathers must determine what their color will be*, he muses, *their shape or the shape plus the opacity of the melanin or other absorptive elements that may be part of them. The throat feathers must all be the same, the crown feathers all the same, though in a wholly different way, otherwise each set could not join forces separately in producing the glittering green gorget and the purple crown.* More spellbound than ever, he thinks of the bird's tiny heart, of its blood, of the infinitesmally small vessels that carry that blood to the developing feathers, and of the forces that determine so finally and—year after year, species by species—so consistently what the shape and color of those feathers is to be. The more he ponders what meets his eye, the more awed he is. *My world*, he muses. *The world I live in! The very special beauty of this tiny part of my world! The fact that I see that beauty, that I feel deeply about it, that I so long to comprehend it!*

The hummingbirds are found only in the Americas. One species breeds as far northward as Alaska, at least one other as far southward as Tierra del Fuego. About fifty species inhabit Mexico, sixteen or so of which are found also in the United States. Very few species are entirely restricted to Mexico. Many Mexican species that do not range as far northward as the United States range southward into Central America and even into South America.

One species in this last category is shown in my drawing, the Green Violet-ear *(Colibri thalasseus)*. This one is found from Jalisco and San Luis Potosí southward to Peru and Bolivia.

The Green Violet-ear I saw only infrequently among the big pines near our camp along the old cobblestone road above Pátzcuaro, Michoacán, in February, 1949. I saw it more often along the edge of the oak woods about a mile west of camp; it seemed commoner still in areas from which all the big trees had been removed. I made my painting along a trail through one of these cleared areas at about 9,000 feet elevation. The plants shown include some tall composites that had gone to seed, flowering lobelia, the leaves of a lupine, and a bit of poison ivy. All of these were just as I found them in one spot beside the trail.

I did not often see a Violet-ear at rest in this open country. When one did alight, it usually twittered. The notes, though sharp, were not very loud.

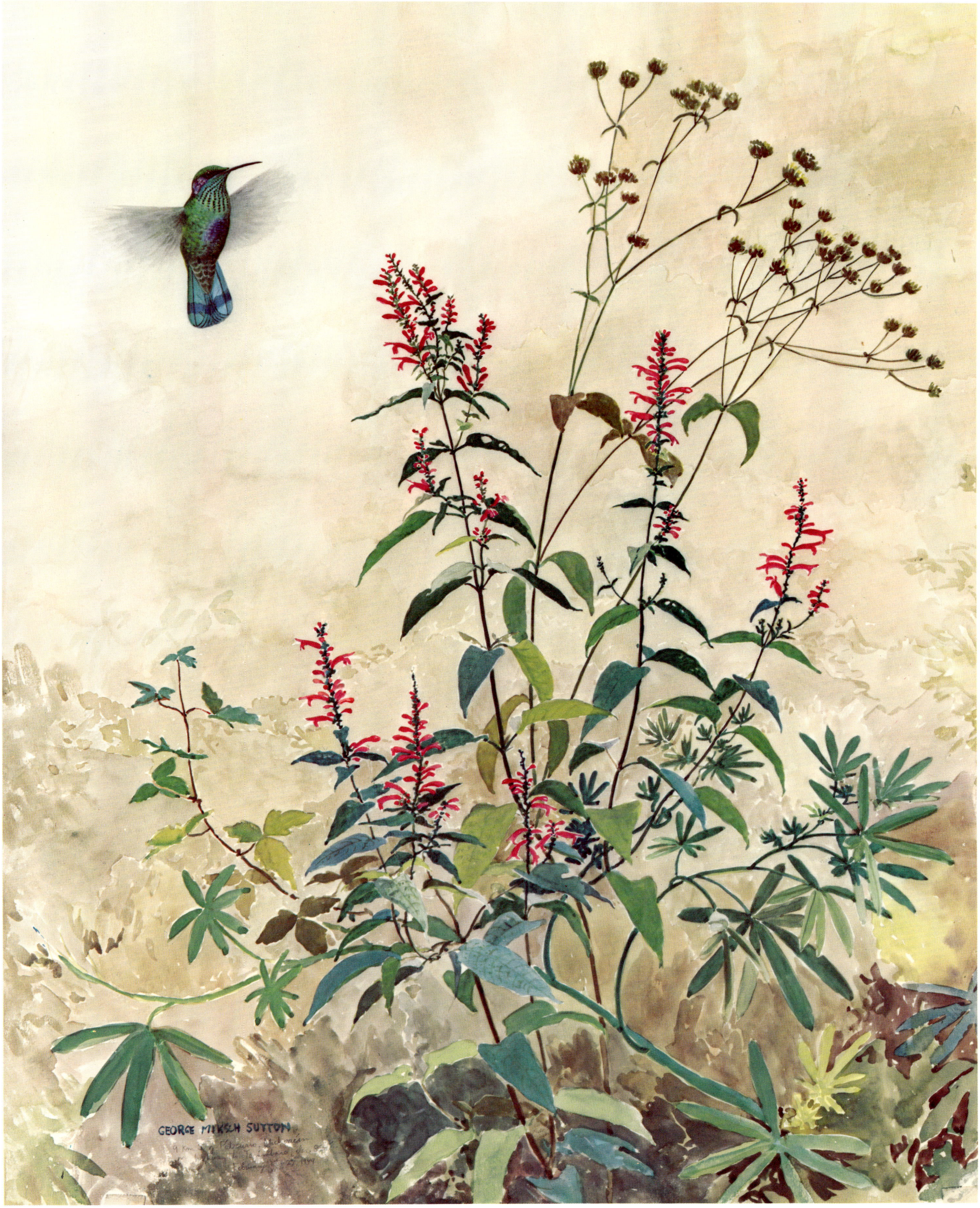
GEORGE MIKSCH SUTTON

MOUNTAIN TROGON

The beauty of the Mountain (or Mexican) Trogon *(Trogon mexicanus)* is at times unbelievable. The iridescent green of its head and upperparts and the red of its underparts are no more gorgeous than those of its low-country cousins, the Elegant Trogon *(T. elegans)* and Collared Trogon *(T. collaris)*; but seen against the somber foliage of oaks and liquidambars at 3,500 feet, of oaks and pines at 8,000 feet, and of firs at 11,000 feet they seem incongruous, out of place. Their incongruity is the more impressive on a cold morning when the observer, rubbing his hands to warm them up, leaves footprints in the frosted grass and finds quiet parts of the stream near camp thinly sheeted with ice. A bird of tropical coloration and affinities in a habitat of this sort? Unbelievable.

Trogon mexicanus ranges from northeastern Mexico southward to Guatemala and Honduras. It is truly montane. Along the Sabinas in southwestern Tamaulipas it has never been seen at river-level so far as I know, though my friends Paul Martin, William Heed, and Richard Robins saw it on the foothill west of the river. There, at about 3,500 feet elevation, Paul Martin found a nest containing two well-feathered young on May 28, 1949. The nest cavity was about 30 feet up in a rotten snag. The plumage of the half-grown nestlings was brown and buff, without a hint of the green and red of the male parent.

I became acquainted with the Mountain Trogon among the big pines and oaks above Pátzcuaro, Michoacán in February, 1949. I did not see much of it there, though I often heard its song—a husky, slowly repeated, slightly plaintive *ka-oh, ka-oh, ka-oh,* in the distance. If, following the sound, I finally found the bird, it stopped singing, voiced its suspicion calling *kuck, kuck, kuck* in a low voice, inspected me with one eye then the other, lifted and spread its tail, then either accepted me and resumed singing or whuffed off rapidly. Its flight was strongly undulatory. Staying well above ground, it found another perch high in a pine. Never did I watch a male without marveling over the intensity of the red of its underparts. No matter how shady the woods or gray the sky, that red fairly glowed. No flower of the area—no orchid, no bromeliad, no begonia—was half so bright.

Two facts about my drawing (made on February 10, 1949, at about 8,500 feet between Pátzcuaro and Tacámbaro, Michoacán) should be stated. First, I did not often see a male and female close together. The sexes usually foraged separately at that season. Second, only occasionally did I see a bird of either sex obtain food from a perched position. As a rule it would fly from a perch to a branch or vine, flutter there while snatching off an insect or berry, and return to the perch before swallowing.

The drawing was not made direct from living models. Before drawing the vine I draped a length of it over a low branch at eye-level. A small gallery of men and boys gathered while I worked. I couldn't send them away, for they were polite and gentle, but when they stood close, hauled chunks of sugar-cane from their pockets, and sharted chewing, I knew that the "moment of truth" was at hand. Pointing to the tiny drops of moisture—spray from the cane—on hand and paper, I pushed everybody back with a look on my face that plainly said, "Now see what you've done!" Actually the spray had worked no evil, but the sound of chewing was more than I could bear while trying to concentrate.

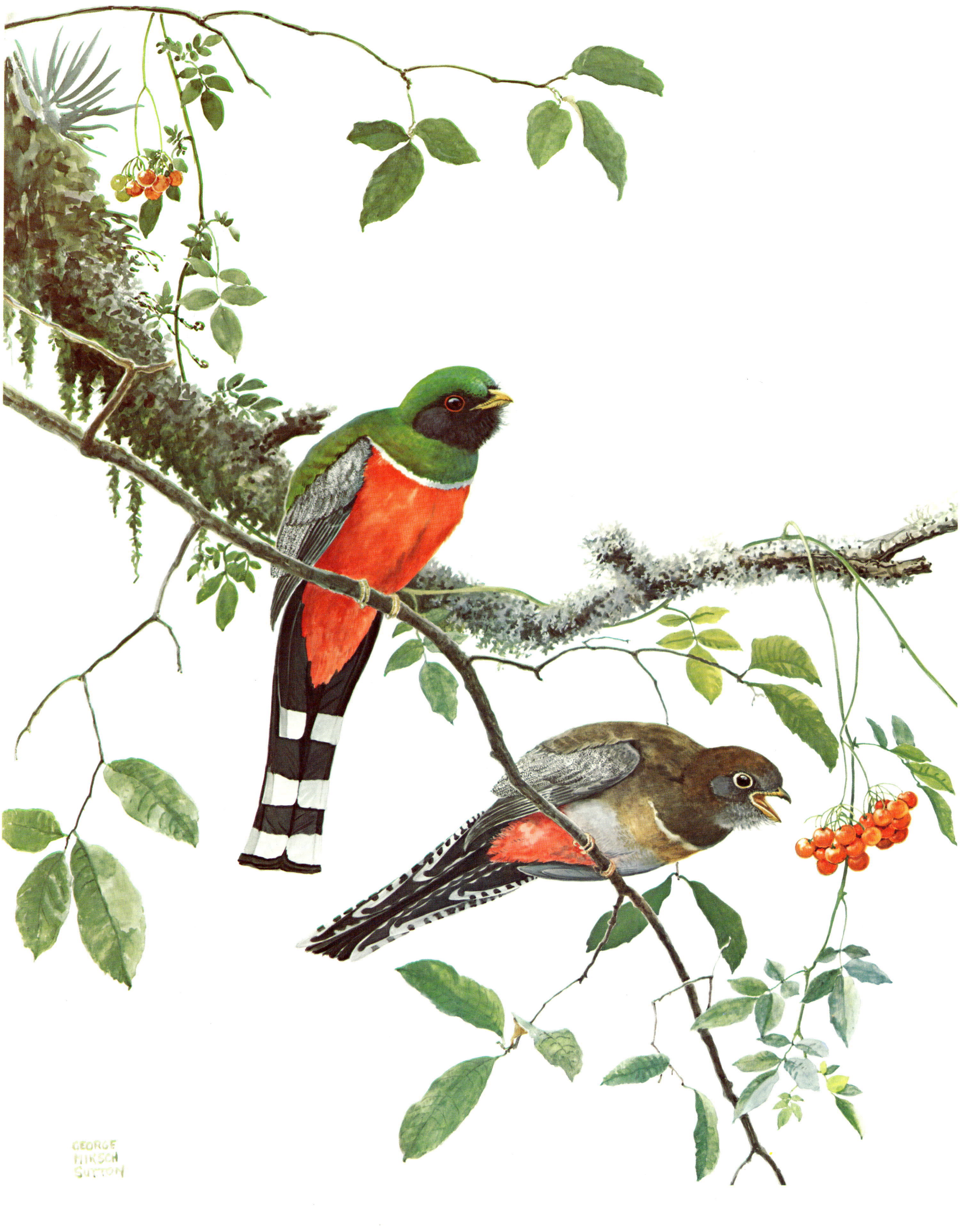
GEORGE MIKSCH SUTTON

ELEGANT TROGON

The Elegant Trogon *(Trogon elegans)* is a well-known Mexican and Central American bird found in brushy woodland in low country and in open pine and oak woods at higher elevations. The two northernmost of the several currently recognized geographical races have long been known as the Coppery-tailed Trogon, because in these forms the middle tail feathers have a rich coppery shine. The middle tail feathers of the southern forms are green, without this coppery tone. The coppery-tailed forms reach their northern limits in Tamaulipas, Nuevo León, Chihuahua, and the mountains of southern Arizona; the green-tailed forms their southern limits in the Tres Marías Islands, Nicaragua, and northwestern Costa Rica.

All the trogons that I know at all well have two "personalities." The perching bird, on the quiet lookout for insects or berries, is almost pensive in manner, turning its head slowly, occasionally lifting and spreading its tail. But let it see food or become alarmed, and it snaps to attention, leans quickly forward, and flips from its perch with wingbeats so powerful as to remind one of a quail or partridge. Close examination of the primary wing feathers shows them to be stiff and strongly curved, in these respects being somewhat like those of a galliform bird.

I first saw the Elegant Trogon on February 17, 1938, not far from the village of Güemes, Tamaulipas. I wrote of the experience thus: "I must have walked five full steps toward that poppy-colored spot before I realized that it was part of a living, breathing bird, a species I had all my life wanted to see. . . . It was perching upright, with tail straight down and underparts toward me. With the glass I could see the narrow snow-white band which separated that incredible red of the belly from the dark shining green of the head and upper chest; the short, conspicuously yellow bill and orange eyelids; the white tail feathers and square tip of the tail. Marveling that I had not frightened it in approaching thus carelessly, I watched it turn its head deliberately as it eyed some object on the ground between us. Its bearing was sluggish, even drowsy.

"The trogon must have recognized the collector in me an instant before I recognized the superb adult male specimen in him, for as I lowered the glass he sprang forward on thumping wings, banked sharply, flashed his white outer tail feathers, and darted off. As he changed course before disappearing, the copper color of his middle tail feathers gleamed brightly."

I was to see much of the Elegant Trogon in eastern Mexico. Its song sounded like *cory, cory, cory, cory*, repeated not very rapidly and reminding me of the slightly plaintive calling of a hen turkey. On April 20, 1941, along the Río Sabinas in southwestern Tamaulipas, I drew my picture. The leaves and berries were done "direct from life"—that is, without breaking the branch off. Alas, nothing in my notes tells me what color the berries became after they had ripened, nor do I know what kind of tree it was.

In mid-May of 1947, Ernest Edwards, Bob Lea, and I watched a pair of Elegant Trogons that probably had a nest in a natural cavity about 40 feet up in a big cypress directly across the Sabinas from our camp at Paño Ayuctle. On May 31 of that year I saw a female bird go into a hole that I had seen a big woodpecker entering only a day or so before. Whose nest-hole was it, the woodpecker's or the trogon's? I did not climb up to find out.

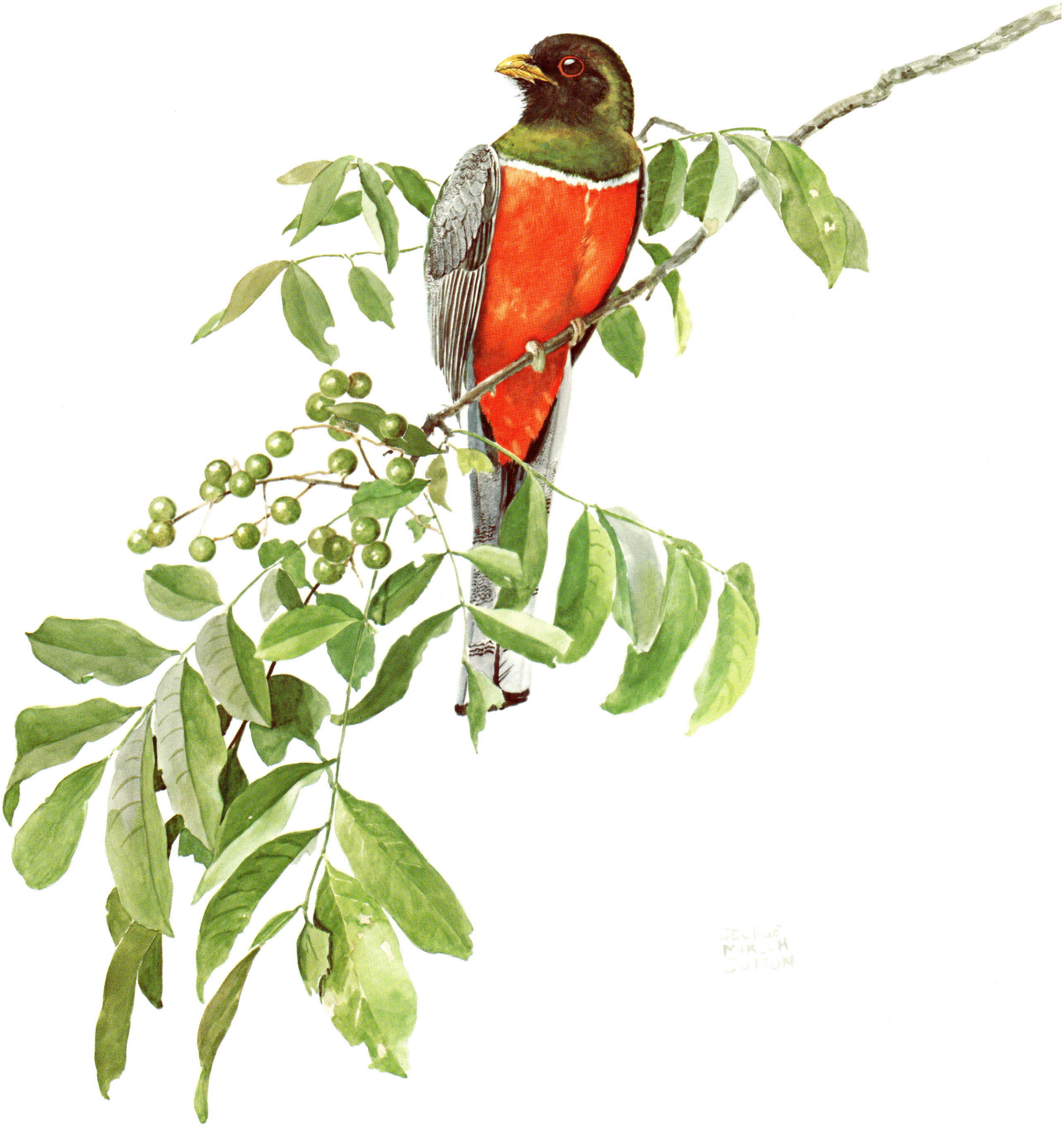

BAR-TAILED TROGON

The bright poppy-red of the underparts of some trogons is an arresting color. Seen against the rich green of tropical verdure or the purple of distant mountains, it hits the eye as few colors do. The light-catching properties of soft plumage may have something to do with the glow that it possesses when seen on the living bird. It seems all the more remarkable when one recalls that it is so very fugitive. Carried by the blood to the developing feathers as a carotenoid pigment, it fades when the dead specimen is exposed continuously to light. If the redness of the feathers is to be preserved, the scientific skins must be kept in the dark. Certain male trogons that have been on display at the University of Oklahoma during the past fifty or more years are so colorless on their underparts that they fail utterly to show what the species looks like in life. In our attempt to restore the color in one specimen we dusted bright red chalk into the belly plumage, a procedure that certainly changed the poor bird's appearance, making it look like a victim of leprosy.

Of the several New World trogons whose underparts are red, the best known is probably the spectacular Quetzal *(Pharomachrus mocinno)*, the national bird of Guatemala, a species that ranges northward into the Mexican states of Chiapas and Oaxaca and that I have never seen alive except in zoos. The upper tail coverts of this bird are so very long that they give the adult male an overall length of about 3 feet. Among the smaller species is the Bar-tailed or Collared Trogon *(Trogon collaris)*, the subject of my painting, a bird found from eastern San Luis Potosí southward to Bolivia and Brazil. This species is about 10 inches long. Its most distinctive feature is the narrowly barred black-and-white three outer pairs of tail feathers in the male. In the female, which I have never painted, the three outer pairs of tail feathers—as seen from underneath—are gray with white tip and narrow black subterminal band.

I made my drawing in the yard of the old original casa at the Hacienda Sabinal near the village of Aquismón, eastern San Luis Potosí, on January 7, 1952. The specimen I used as a model had been collected along a trail in the "big woods." I worked with it while it was still quite fresh, of course, and was struck not so much with the clear yellow of its bill—for I had noticed that in the field—as with the dull grayness of the eyelids. I had expected them to outline the eye clearly, as they do in the Elegant Trogon (*T. elegans*), but this they did not do. Bar-tailed Trogons that I had seen that day called *kyook, kyook, kyook* in a husky voice.

The strange plant that I decided to show in my drawing is an orchid that had long since finished blooming. It was not far above the ground, so I did not have to climb for it. Climbing was to be avoided, for I wanted to keep my hands in good shape for drawing.

GEORGE MIKSCH SUTTON
Rancho Sabinal, San Luis Potosí
January 8, 1952

BLUE-CROWNED MOTMOT

One of the delightful sounds of the lowland woods of eastern Mexico is the *poot-poot* of the Blue-crowned Motmot *(Momotus momota)*, a bird of the New World tropics found northward to Tamaulipas and Nuevo León. The call is so soft when heard at a distance that it brings to mind the hooting of a small owl. Often it is so faint a part of the medley of bird voices that it escapes detection. If, on the other hand, it is heard in a deep, closed-in, shadowy gully near the motmot's nest burrow, it may have an almost explosive quality. Find the bird and watch it. Note the rich olive-green and blue of its upperparts as it moves from perch to perch. On alighting it swings its long tail slowly from side to side. Its bright eyes are red or red-orange.

That tail deserves discussion. Only the two middle feathers, considerably the longest of the ten, are racket-tipped. When those two first grow out they are "normal," i.e., there are barbs at each side of the shaft from base to tip. But as a result of wear and tear, and possibly of preening, the barbs of a narrowed part 2 to 3 inches back from the tip break off, leaving an inch-long stretch of bare shaft between the basal 6 inches and the racket-shaped distal end. I wish I could say that I have seen a motmot picking those barbs off with its bill, but I can't. Indeed, I have never visited Mexico at the right season for witnessing behavior of this particular sort. If motmots preen those tail feathers into a racket-tipped condition, they almost certainly do it shortly after the annual molt into fresh plumage has been completed. That time would be late summer, after the breeding season.

I do know, however, that the birds have a rough time of it digging the nest burrow, a long tunnel used throughout the period of egg-laying, incubation, and fledging. Whether they back out of their burrow while digging it, I cannot say. After it is finished they regularly come out head-first, and this means that they have to turn around, long tail and all, somewhere back there in the dark, and this is bound to be hard on the tail, especially those long middle feathers. By the end of the breeding season many a Blue-crowned Motmot's tail is a sorry sight. Some birds that I have watched carrying food to the burrow were stub-tailed. A Blue-crowned Motmot's tail is about 9 inches long most of the year, but hard-working parent birds sometimes have worn-off tails only half that length.

The nest burrow is usually in a vertical bank. One that I found in the early spring of 1941 was in a hard, rather dry chunk of earth adhering to the roots of a big fallen tree. The excited birds called *poot-poot* as I approached and sat down, intending to watch from a distance; but when I moved up to examine the burrow they squawked and grunted as they darted at me.

My drawing was made on March 25, 1941. It shows a female bird on a branch to which cling some of those strangely artificial-looking bromeliads.

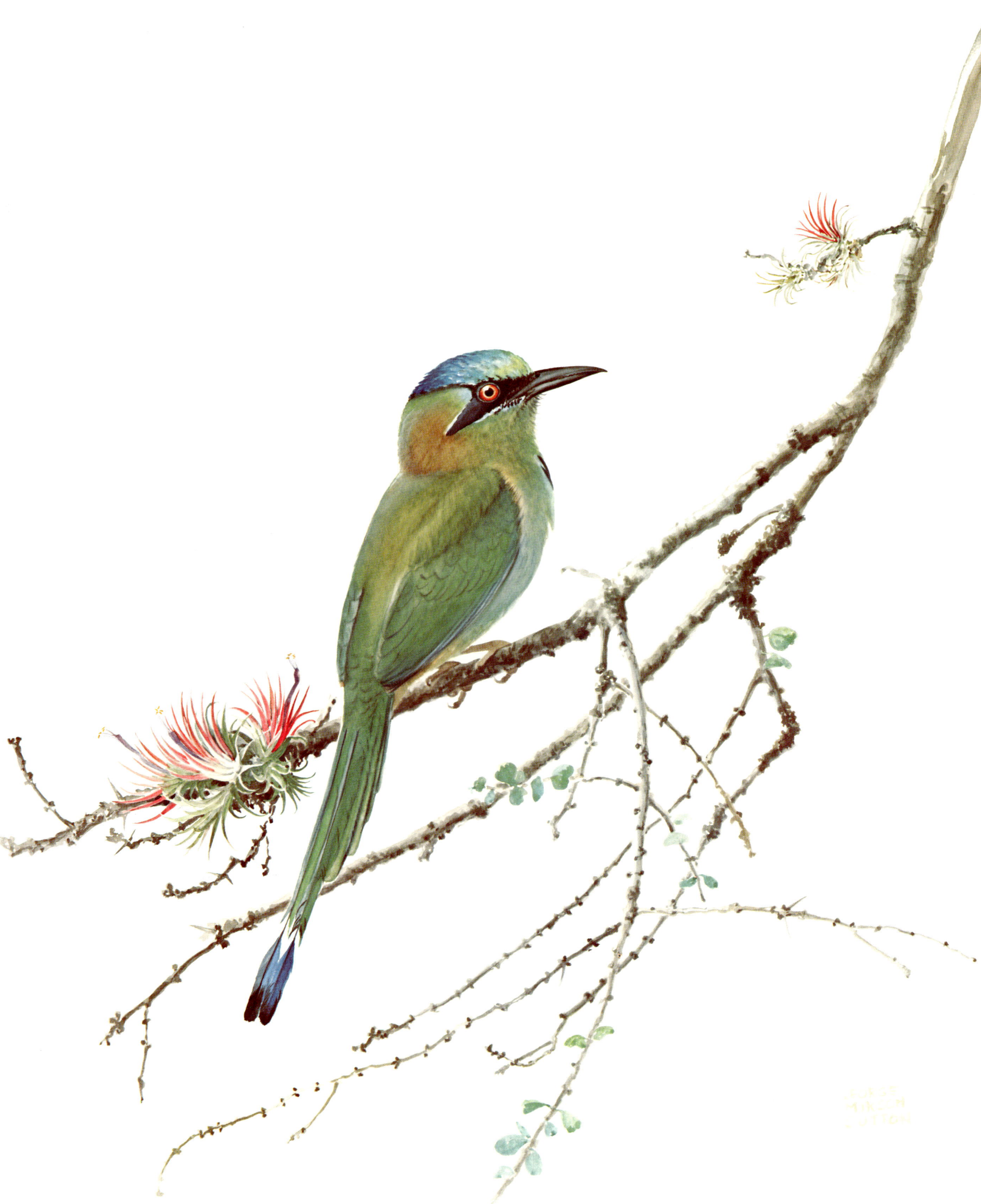

RINGED KINGFISHER

The rivers of Mexico are fairly alive with kingfishers. The largest of them, the Ringed Kingfisher (*Megaceryle torquata*), a big-billed bird about 15 inches long, ranges from the Lower Río Grande Valley, where it is rare, and from southern Sinaloa southward throughout continental parts of the New World and the Lesser Antilles as far as Tierra del Fuego. The next largest, the Amazon Kingfisher *(Chloroceryle amazona)*, a crested, green-backed species about 11 inches long, is found from southern Tamaulipas and southern Sinaloa southward to Peru and central Argentina. The Green Kingfisher *(C. americana)*, which is only about half as bulky as the Amazon, is found from southern Texas and northern Sonora southward to Peru and Argentina. Smallest of all is the Pygmy Kingfisher *(C. aenea)*, a midget little more than 5 inches long, found from Veracruz, Oaxaca, and Yucatán southward to Ecuador, Bolivia, and southern Brazil. The four species just named are largely, if not wholly, nonmigratory. In winter a species from the United States and Canada, the Belted Kingfisher *(Megaceryle alcyon)*, invades the whole of Mexico, crowding things somewhat.

In southern Mexico, where all five of these kingfishers live side by side in winter, competition for food must be fierce, since not one of the five subsists at all exclusively on food captured away from water as certain kingfishers of the Old World do. The Pygmy Kingfisher is said to eat aquatic insects as well as little fish; the Green Kingfisher catches minnows that its larger cousins probably spurn; the Belted and Amazon kingfishers no doubt catch frogs and crayfish as well as fish; and the big Ringed Kingfisher probably does not waste energy catching anything but fairly large fish, large frogs, and snakes that expose themselves swimming across streams. Thus fitting themselves together ecologically, all five kingfishers manage to survive. One possible prey species I continue to wonder about, the slim gar, an armored fish that is common in many Mexican rivers. I have seen gars repeatedly along the Sabinas, always big ones. Do kingfishers of any species catch young gars? If so, they must be exceedingly sharp-eyed, for young gars, drifting along like debris just beneath the surface, usually escape detection. Drifting along and looking like dead leaves is *their* means of surviving. I find myself wondering whether the big gars occasionally turn the tables, so to speak, and capture the kingfishers. They look quite capable of such reciprocity.

Ringed Kingfishers were not common along the Sabinas in January of 1949, but I saw and heard two or three of the fine birds every day. I noticed that they usually flew several feet above the water, whereas the little "greens" almost invariably kept within inches of the river's bosom, as if aware of the fact that they could dive to safety *instantly* if attacked from above. Occasionally the Ringed Kingfishers flew a hundred feet or so up, but always they followed the river's course. They, too, sensed that the river itself was their habitat, that to leave the river might be a mistake. How I enjoyed the rough *ke-rack* or *ka-dack* that announced the big kingfisher's passing.

I made my drawing on January 19. That day I saw at least three Ringed Kingfishers in a territorial wrangle above the river, one Belted Kingfisher, and a half dozen or so of the "little greens."

(From the collection of Dr. and Mrs. Robert H. Furman)

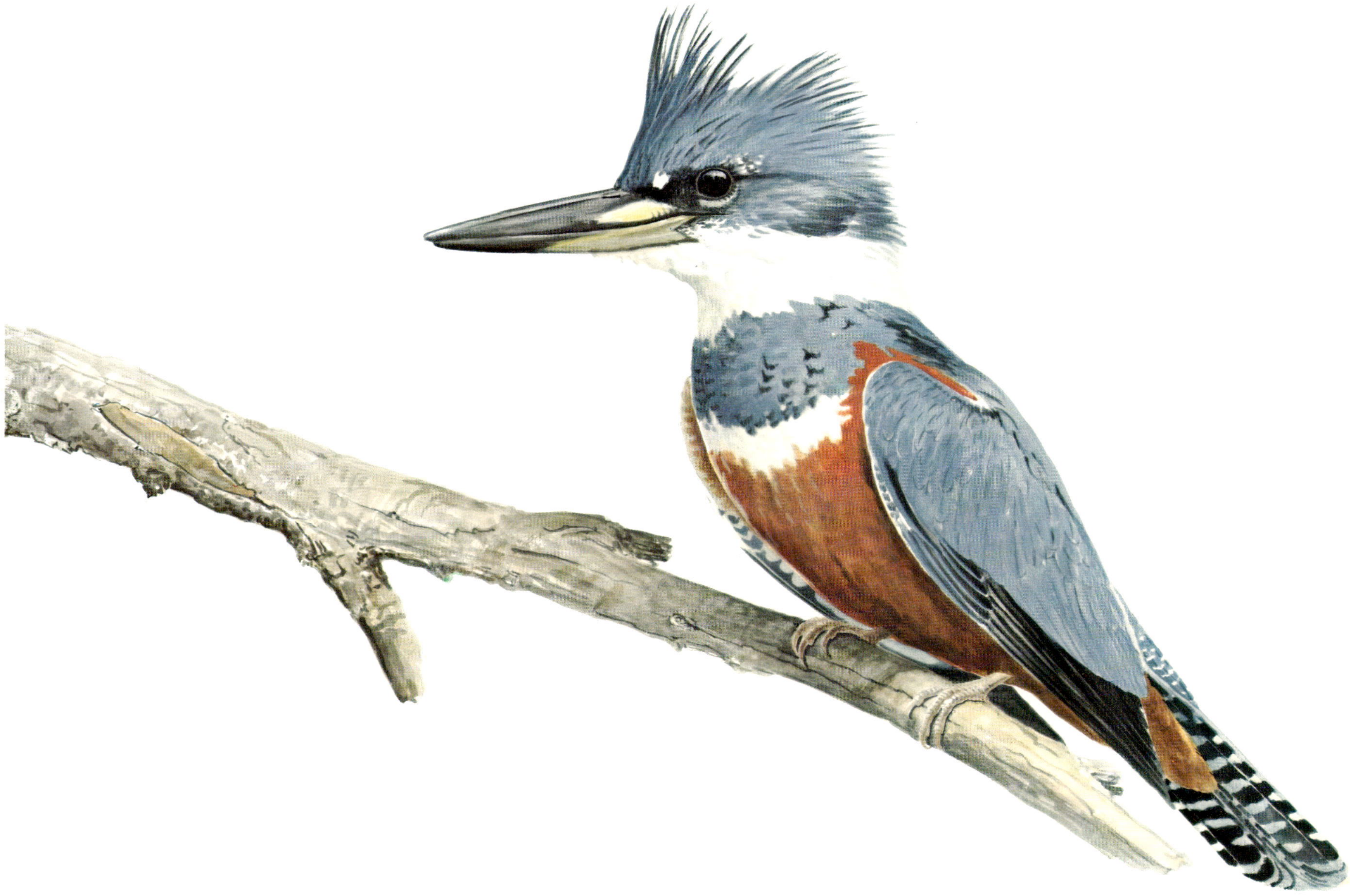

BRONZE-WINGED WOODPECKER

Among oaks and pines on slopes well above the city of Monterrey, Nuevo León, in mid-February of 1938, I saw my first Bronze-winged Woodpecker *(Piculus aeruginosus)*, a handsome species found only in eastern Mexico. Our base at the time was the Mesa de Chipinque, a broad shelf on the north side of the mountain. We were at the northernmost tip of the bird's range, and I continue to wonder why it was so exclusively montane there. Could the nights on the mountain conceivably have been warmer than at Monterrey-level? So far as I know, the species has never been reported from woodland in the low country just north of Monterrey, yet later in the season in 1938 we found it at much lower elevation in heavy woods along the west edge of the coastal plain in central and southern Tamaulipas.

Those first Bronze-winged Woodpeckers of my experience lived at elevations ranging from 4,000 to about 7,000 feet. Their most characteristic call was so flickerlike that I misidentified it and in consequence had to re-write several of my notes. The bird's habit of perching on a horizontal branch with tail not propped against the bark but hanging straight down, also was flickerlike. The head of a male specimen that Tom Burleigh collected on February 12, I sketched that day in watercolor. A colored reproduction of the drawing appeared in my book *Mexican Birds*.

In the spring of 1941 my party found the Bronze-winged Woodpecker uncommon along the Río Sabinas in southwestern Tamaulipas. There it had considerable elevational range, for we saw it not only at river-level but well up on the foothill. On March 27, Dwain Warner collected a male specimen at a recently-finished hole about 25 feet above ground at the top of a stub in mixed woods near the river. This bird I painted. On April 18, I observed a pair of the birds prancing, bowing, and spreading wings and tail precisely as flickers might have, and their calls were decidedly flickerlike.

On April 24, Sewall Pettingill found a nest in a stub across the river from the house, watched the pair changing places at the nest entrance, and decided to take movies of them. Although the Sabinas was on a rampage, there was no way to stop the photographer. Sewall will never forget how some of his equipment got across. Señora Rodriguez, wife of our chief factotum, knew that the camera had to be taken to the other side so—quite without discussing the matter with Pettingill—she just put it on her head and started. Pettingill didn't even know what had happened until the capable Señora was halfway across. He had the good sense to say not a word of warning and she the equipoise to get to the other side safely. Having put her precious burden down, she smiled broadly. Pettingill, thoroughly shaken but profoundly grateful, could only smile broadly in return—from his side of the river.

A nest found by Paul S. Martin on May 27, 1949, at 3,300 feet elevation at Frank Harrison's wonderful Rancho del Cielo, was about 40 feet up in a dead liquidambar. It contained at least three well-developed young birds not yet quite ready to fledge.

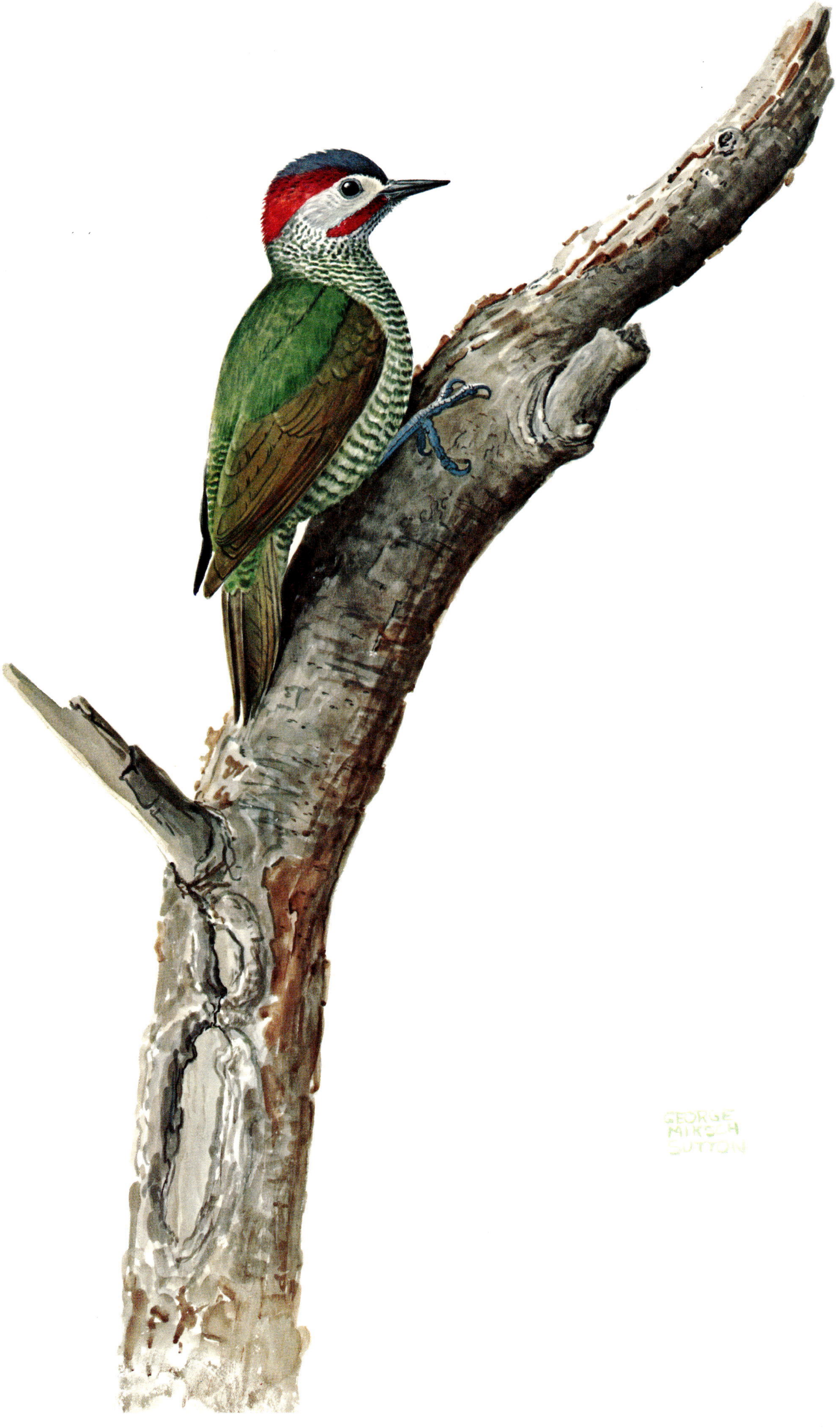
GEORGE
MIKSCH
SUTTON

IVORY-BILLED WOODCREEPER

During the first few days of March in 1938, along the Río Sabinas in southwestern Tamaulipas, I made the acquaintance of the Ivory-billed Woodcreeper *(Xiphorhynchus flavigaster)*, the northernmost member of the great New World woodcreeper family. I first saw the species on February 28. We must have been at the north edge of its range there, for we had not seen it along the Río Corona near Ciudad Victoria. Its northern limits in western Mexico are in southeastern Sonora. Its southern limits are in northwestern Costa Rica.

Thus did I write, in *Mexican Birds*, about my first glimpse of an Ivory-billed Woodcreeper: "A muffled tapping attracted my attention to a tree just across the trail. There, clinging to a horizontal bough, was a streaked brown bird somewhat smaller than a flicker, busily investigating a tangle of orchid roots. Dismissing me with a glance and the roots with a jab of its beak, it hitched along toward the main trunk, using its tail woodpecker-wise, as a prop."

I was soon to learn that a foraging Ivory-billed Woodcreeper usually keeps to the main trunk, moving upward hurriedly, passing most of the branches by, picking at the bark, prying pieces loose, but never working very long at a certain spot or attempting to dig a hole. On reaching the point where the trunk becomes small or the bark smooth, it drops to the base of the next tree and starts another climb. It is not at all noticeable while climbing, and when it drops from one tree to another it resembles a dead leaf falling; but just before it alights it spreads its rufous-brown wings and swoops upward, becoming quite conspicuous for just an instant. On many occasions I became aware of the bird's presence through seeing the bright brown flash of those widespread wings. Some of the bird's cries were like those of a flicker— a circumstance that did not help much, for the cries of the Bronze-winged Woodpecker *(Piculus aeruginosus)* also sounded like those of a flicker. The woodcreeper's song was a series of loud, far-carrying notes that reminded me of the down-the-scale song of a Canyon Wren *(Catherpes mexicanus)*.

The only Ivory-billed Woodcreeper nest I have ever seen was found by one of our Mexican friends at the end of a narrow island in the Sabinas River. It was in a natural cavity between the "arm" of a strangling fig and the trunk of a cypress, about 4½ feet from the ground. When found on May 25, 1947, it held two pure white, not very glossy eggs. On the following day it held three, the complete clutch. The nest itself was a mass of bark chips about 3 inches deep. While we were at the nest one bird scolded continuously, its cry of alarm being a sharp *wheedle* or *feed-ler*.

I made my drawing at Paño Ayuctle along the Río Sabinas during the last week of January, 1949. I started out with the trunk of the big cypress and the "arms" of the *huigerón* (strangling fig) that clasped it so tightly. I worked by spells, two or three hours at a stretch, sitting on a stool made from a section of tree trunk topped with a board. Literally for days the drawing had a leprous appearance, for I left completely blank the space that would eventually hold the bird figure. We finally caught a specimen in the mist-net, and I completed the drawing—much to the relief of everyone.

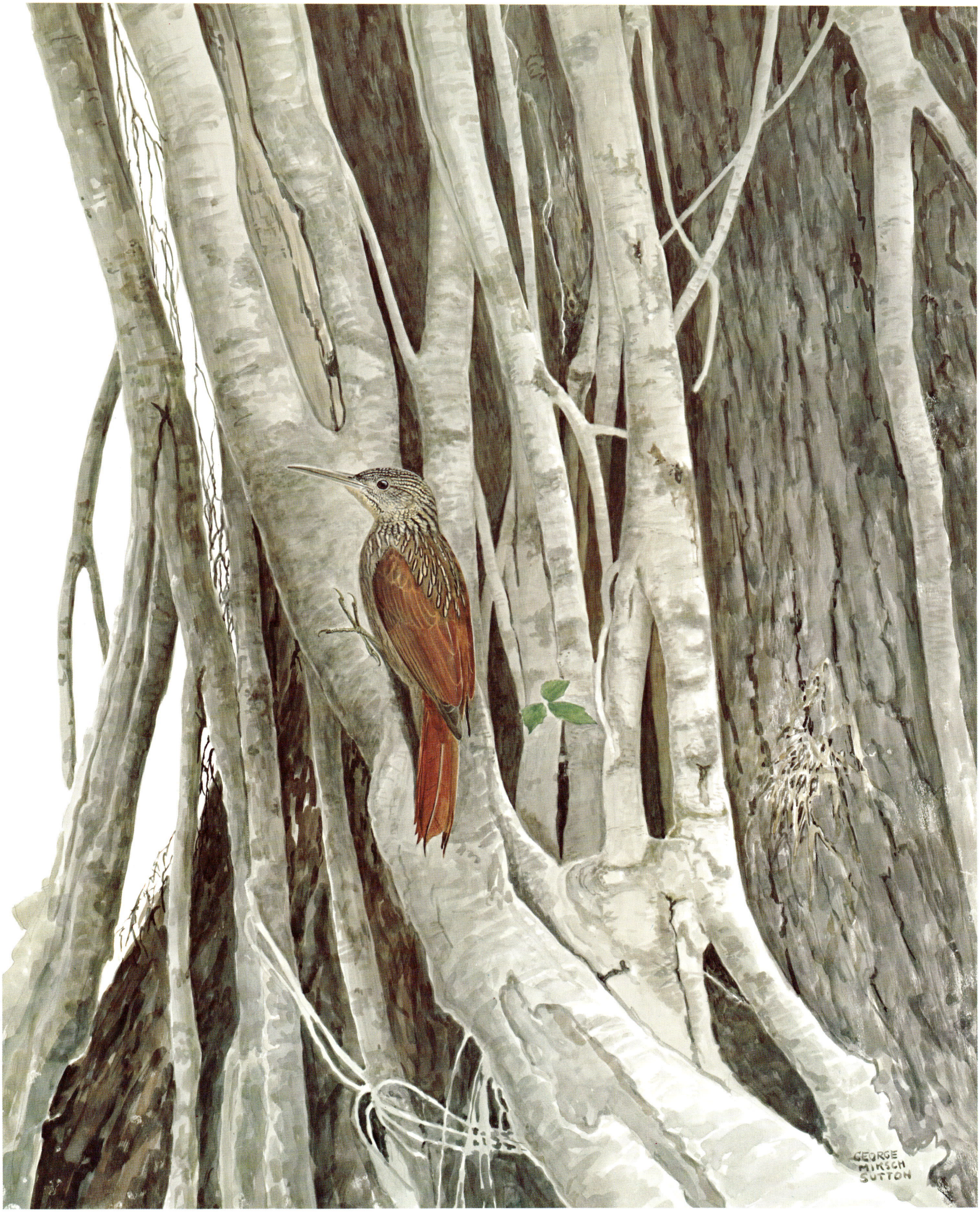
GEORGE
MIKSCH
SUTTON

MASKED TITYRA

Calling the Masked Tityra *(Tityra semifasciata)* a kind of cotinga may not help much toward identifying it. A cotinga is a member of the New World Family Cotingidae, a heterogeneous group of very small (3½ inches) to fairly large (20 inches) arboreal birds found principally in the tropics. Among the ninety species is the spectacular Umbrella Bird *(Cephalopterus ornatus)* of South America. The most northern of them all, the Rose-throated Becard *(Platypsaris aglaiae)*, ranges from Costa Rica northward to southern Texas and southern Arizona.

The Masked Tityra is a somewhat stocky bird 8 inches long that ranges from Bolivia and Brazil northward to Tamaulipas and Sonora. Nowhere does it quite reach the United States. It is a creature of strange facial expression, for its dark eye is surrounded by a sizeable area of thickish, featherless, raspberry-red skin. The basal half of the bill is of the same shade of red. The bill is heavy and slightly hooked. Only the male bird wears the black mask. In the female the upperparts are brown rather than gray.

I have seen a good deal of the Masked Tityra in southwestern Tamaulipas along the northern edge of its range. The only call I have heard from it was a short, dry, wholly unmusical *quert*—often the single syllable, sometimes a terse repetition. I heard the sound many times before realizing that it was not from a large insect or tree-frog.

When we began our work along the Río Sabinas in March of 1941 some Masked Tityras were going about in pairs, but we often saw a group of three or four birds perching drowsily in a leafless treetop, then suddenly chasing each other about. What we interpreted as courtship included snapping off and presentation of twigs, accompanied by head-wagging and grunting. About the first of April, nesting began. From then on, pairs were the rule, and we often saw them perched side by side near natural cavities or old woodpecker holes. On April 10 we watched a female bird as she carried forty-two twigs to a hole in half an hour. At this nest only the female worked; but on April 17, at a natural cavity in another tree, both the male and the female removed twigs. They tossed these away rather than carrying them to another cavity. From April 4 to 8, a pair near our house fought fiercely with Golden-fronted Woodpeckers *(Centurus aurifrons)* over a nest-hole the woodpeckers were doing their best to finish. They could do no digging while the tityras were trying to take possession. The woodpeckers called loudly as they fought, but all we heard from the tityras was that gruntlike *quert*. After four wearisome days of fighting, the woodpeckers won out.

My drawing shows a male bird perched on a flowering branch of the tree our Mexican friends called the *palo de rosa*. The flowers appeared before the leaves did. When all the blossoms were fully out the tree was a truly glorious sight. To obtain a model for me to paint from, Bob Lea climbed up, carefully cut a flowering branch, and let it down with a rope. The scientific name of the tree is *Tabebuia pentaphylla*.

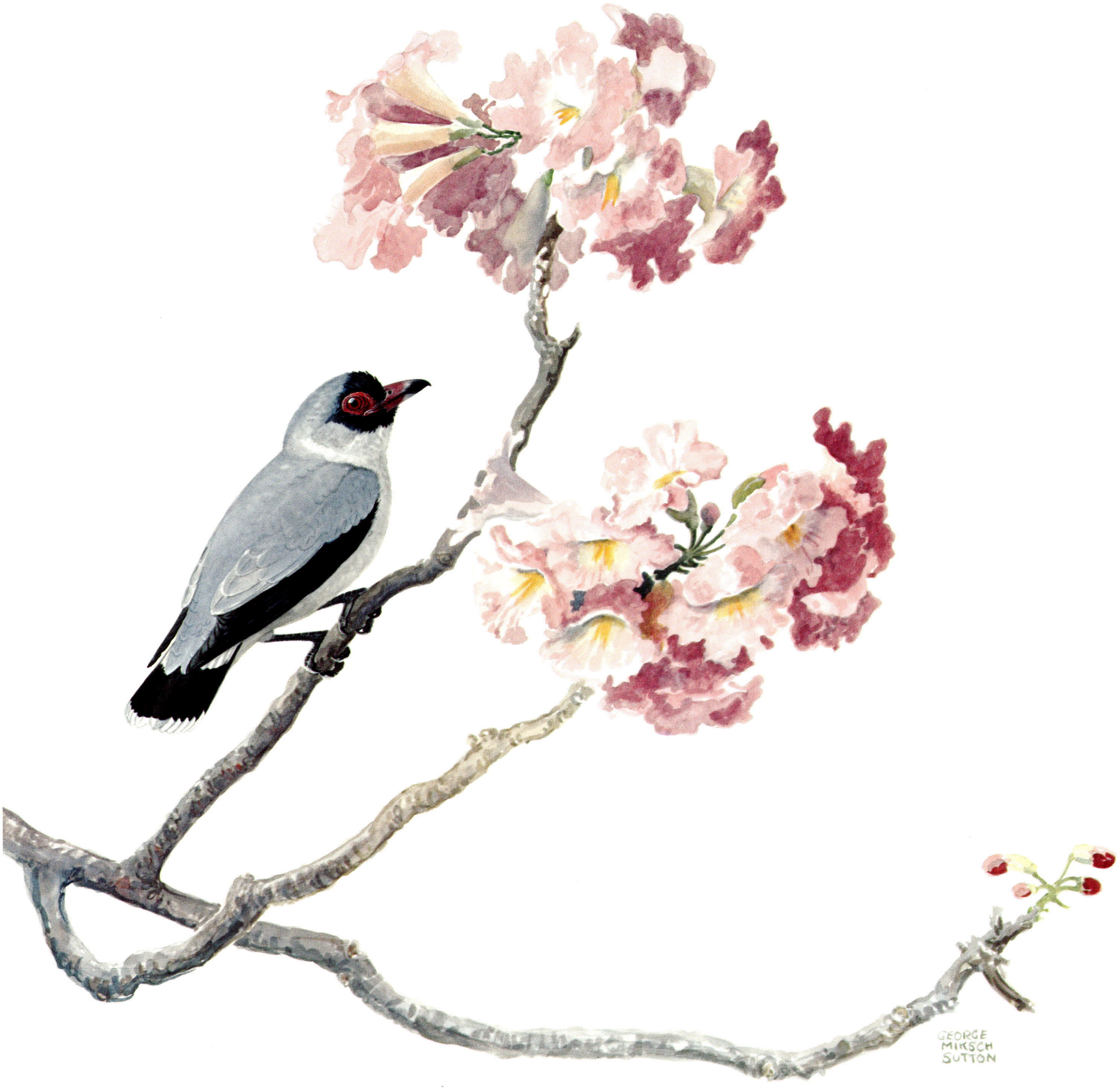
GEORGE
MIKSCH
SUTTON

BOAT-BILLED FLYCATCHER

Bird students unfamiliar with the birdlife of Mexico are sure to be impressed by the bewildering similarity of certain species to each other. Sometimes the "lookalikes" are closely related, but often they are not. Yellow-breasted birds a little smaller than robins seen perched on telephone wires along highways and in towns almost anywhere in low parts of Mexico are likely to be Tropical Kingbirds *(Tyrannus melancholicus)*. But in wilder areas—away from roads and wires—the yellow-breasted birds one is likely to see range in size from the little stub-tailed tanagers known as euphonias to the somewhat larger Social Flycatcher *(Myiozetetes similis)*, the still larger Tropical Kingbird, and the two big-as-robins flycatchers known as the Kiskadee (*Pitangus sulphuratus*) and the Boat-billed Flycatcher (*Megarynchus pitangua*). All these yellow-breasted birds (not to mention others) have a tantalizing way of getting together in a tree along a river and sitting quietly there in the early morning sunlight daring the beginner to identify them correctly.

Of the species just mentioned, the two most northward ranging are the Tropical Kingbird, which breeds from southwestern Arizona and southern Texas southward through Mexico and Central and South America to Bolivia and Argentina, and the Kiskadee, which has about the same over-all range, though its northern limits in the west are in southern Sonora.

As the beginner travels southward in Mexico his real troubles start in Sinaloa and southern Tamaulipas, where the Boat-billed Flycatcher enters the picture. Here is a fine, big bird that looks for all the world like a Kiskadee but that has a much heavier bill, that is not rufous on its wings and tail but olive instead, and that does not perch on rocks in a stream and dive for minnows as the Kiskadee does. Both species are noisy. The Kiskadee's loud, far-carrying *geep-career* is instantly recognizable. (I recall being comforted by the fact that I knew just which bird was making it when I heard it among the welter of calls that I did *not* recognize along the Amazon!) The Boat-bill's most characteristic cry is a rough, grating, somewhat peevish sounding *kair-r-r-r* or *keer-r-r-r*, which sometimes is lengthened to *te-keer-r-r-r*, or *tay-kair-r-r-r*. I have heard also such phrases as *kee-wick*, *kree-kilrick*, and *ki-zeedick*.

Between April 7 and the end of the month in 1941 we found several Boat-bill nests, each a rather shallow, thinly lined cup of twigs placed in an open crotch or on a horizontal branch—one in a cypress, one in a silk-cotton tree, the highest of the several that we knew of, about 25 feet up. How wholly unlike the big, domed-over, ball-like Kiskadee nests they were! The birds were very deliberate in their nest-building. I recall in particular one pair that had a partly finished nest close to a trail. When a small hawk happened by, the flycatchers both took after it in a rage, giving cries that I could find no human syllables for, snapping their bills fiercely.

My painting shows a male bird in a silk-cotton tree whose flowers had a curiously twirled appearance. I made the painting in the early spring of 1941.

64

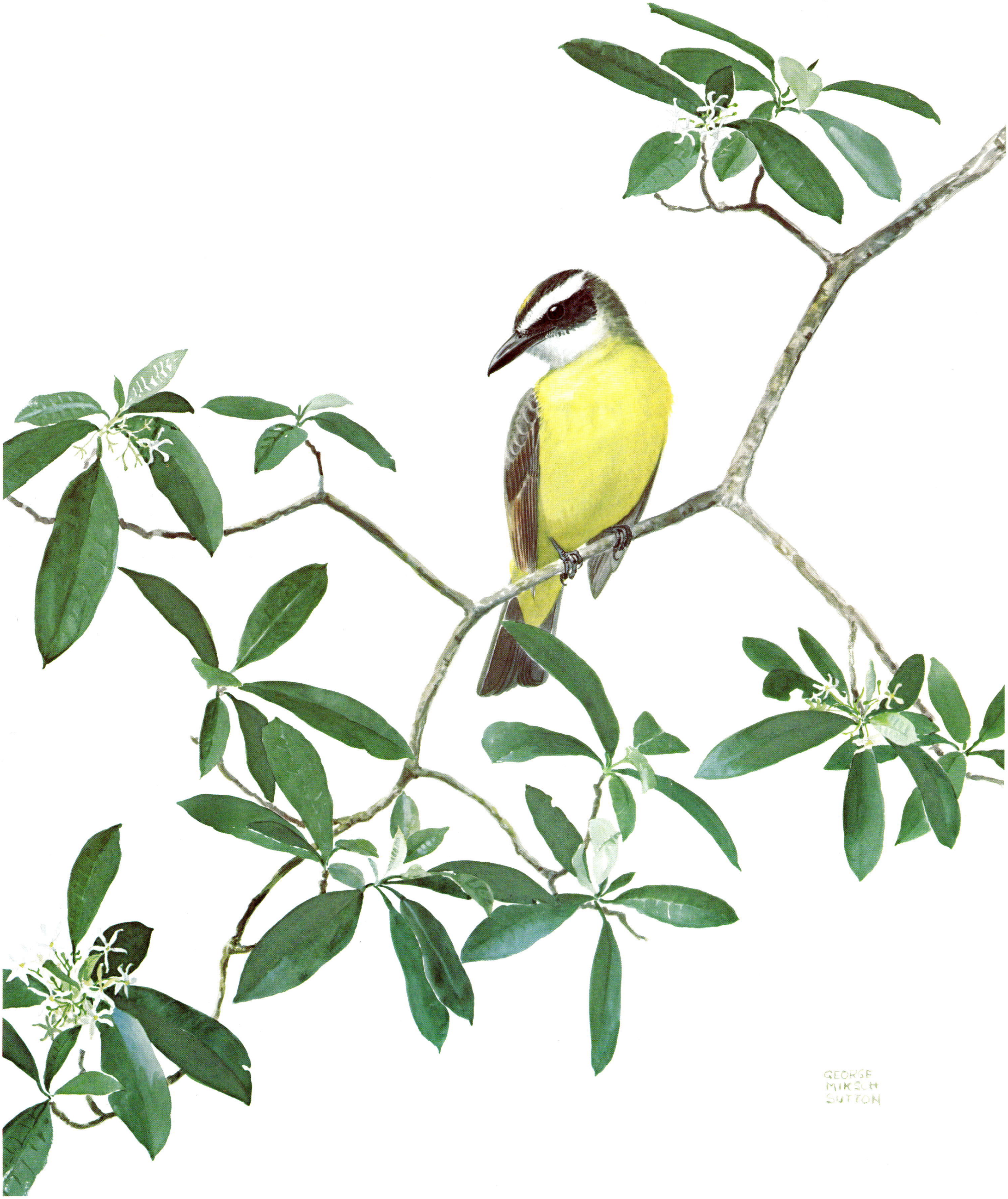
GEORGE
MIKSCH
SUTTON

BEARDLESS FLYCATCHER

One of Mexico's least noticeable birds is the dull-colored, 4-inch-long Beardless Flycatcher *(Camptostoma imberbe)*, a species so often called "nondescript" that I take this occasion to rise in protest. To be sure, the little thing is an unexciting olive gray above and dingy white below. It has neither conspicuous eyering nor bold wingbars. Its odd little *pee-yuk* is not much of a call note, nor is the *ee, ee, ee, ee, ee* that it emits now and then much of a song, but it is a winsome creature, even so, especially when it lifts its rather long crown feathers, making them a crest.

I sometimes wonder whether *Camptostoma imberbe* is truly a flycatcher. Its name calls attention to the fact that it has no rictal bristles—equipment that most "true" flycatchers possess. Furthermore, it is not given to perching upright and sallying forth after winged insects in traditional flycatcher style. As it moves about among the twigs it reminds one strongly not of a phoebe or a pewee but of a kinglet, warbler, or vireo. Its bill is not broad and flat, like that of most flycatchers.

The Beardless Flycatcher is found in semiarid lowland thickets from southern Texas and southeastern Arizona southward to Costa Rica. I have seen it principally in the Lower Río Grande Valley in Texas and in Tamaulipas and Nuevo León.

Keeping after a bird diligently enough to learn its ways is certain to endear it to oneself. For years I had been paying special attention to the pre-dawn singing of the flycatchers of the New World Family Tyrannidae. As a youngster in Nebraska I had heard Eastern Kingbirds *(Tyrannus tyrannus)*, the birds we kids called "bee martins," singing in the early morning darkness high in air. In Oklahoma I had often been charmed by the early morning *pit, pit, pit-a-tip* calls of Scissor-tailed Flycatchers *(Muscivora forficata)*. In Mexico, it took work, real work, to locate Beardless Flycatchers along a trail in late evening, to figure out about where they'd be roosting, and to ascertain the following morning that they sang before dawn. Imagine my excitement and satisfaction when I heard an unfamiliar song, jotted down at the time as *chew-did-ee, chew-did-see*, repeated over and over, thirty times or more, from the top of a not very large, thinly-leafed tree and found—when there was light enough for me to see the singer—that it was a Beardless Flycatcher. During the last week in April and in early May my companions and I were to hear that sunrise song daily. On April 21 we discovered an unfinished nest about 25 feet up in a big cypress at the river's edge. Both birds of the pair seemed to be at work, but I was not sure that both were gathering material. Indeed I could not see the nest itself, for it was in the very middle of a long scarf of moss (Sutton, 1942, *Auk*, 59: 23).

My drawing, made on April 25, 1941, shows a singing male perched in a flowering cassia tree. I did the branch direct from the tree beside the road between our house at the Rancho Rinconada and the main highway. Note, in particular, the little bird's raised crest and yellow mouth lining.

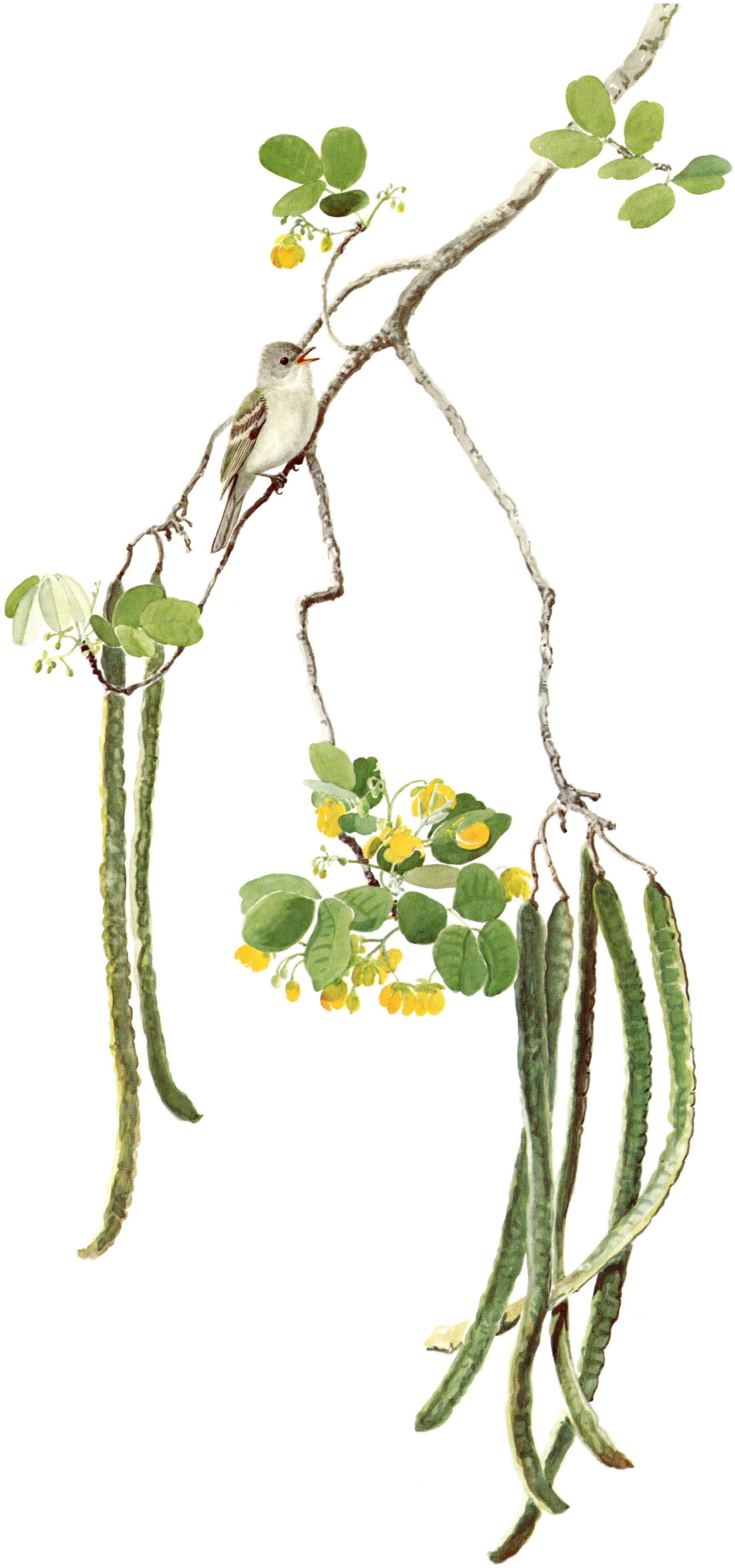

MAGPIE-JAY

In the vicinity of the Hacienda el Cóbano, about 6 miles north of the old city of Colima, in southwestern Mexico, the Magpie-Jay *(Calocitta formosa)* is well known but uncommon. "Oh yes, there are lots of them around here," said the enthusiastic, warm-hearted Mexicans, "we call them *urracas*." Yet during my stay in mid-January of 1971 I did not see or hear one of the birds, and in the latter half of May in 1973 I considered myself fortunate when I found a pair and their recently fledged young in a tangle of woods within a quarter of a mile of the hacienda buildings.

Happening upon these five big jays was a memorable experience. Along a much-used path that led between woods and sugar-cane field, I was often bewildered by the songs and alarm notes of birds I did not know well. A clearly enunciated *chuck-pree* proved to be from a Gray Saltator *(Saltator coerulescens)*, actually a song I had heard many times before, in eastern Mexico. A very loud, complex song that I felt sure was that of a wren continued to bewilder me. This invariably came from the depths of a thicket well back from the path, so I had to climb a stone wall, listen again, move forward a few steps, listen again, and thus proceed a few yards at a time in hopes of seeing the singer. Most of the time during approaches of this sort I was fairly well hidden—another way of saying that, from where I was, not much of the sky was visible. At one point, however, I stepped into the open, noticed a shadow moving swiftly toward me, and looked up to see a wide-winged, long-tailed bird swooping swiftly at my head. At a distance of about 3 feet the 2-feet-long creature gave a squawk that made me jump in my tracks. As it veered upward I could see that its outer tail feathers were white-tipped. Its loud call summoned its mate. The two birds set the woods to ringing with their alarum. It didn't take long for me to sense that I had invaded their nest territory. Utterly unrelenting in their attacks, they swung back and forth over me, squawking, giving me glorious looks at the grayish blue, white, and black of their plumage. When they alighted close by and squawked in my direction, the long, black, recurved feathers of their crests shook jauntily.

Presently I saw the young ones, all about as large as their parents, but stub-tailed. They were about 30 feet up in a large tree. Two of them were perching quietly, close together, with plumage fluffed out comfortably and feet hidden, the picture of innocence. The third, a slightly longer-tailed individual on a branch several feet above them, was heeding the cries of its parents and moving off awkwardly. I decided that not one of the brood could fly well. A big nest, that appeared to be about the size of a crow's, was on one of the tree's highest branches, perhaps 70 feet up. I had no way of knowing, of course, that the young birds had been reared in that nest, but I guessed that they had.

The female bird in my drawing obviously is excited. I had a hard time choosing accessory material—leaves, berries, etc.—that would in no way compete with, or detract from, the jay. All of the leaves were drawn directly from parts of plants brought to the patio of the main building at the hacienda. There in the "grateful shade," with a gentle breeze blowing, I was wonderfully comfortable as I worked. And not a tick anywhere!

(From the collection of Dr. and Mrs. Guy M. Anthony)

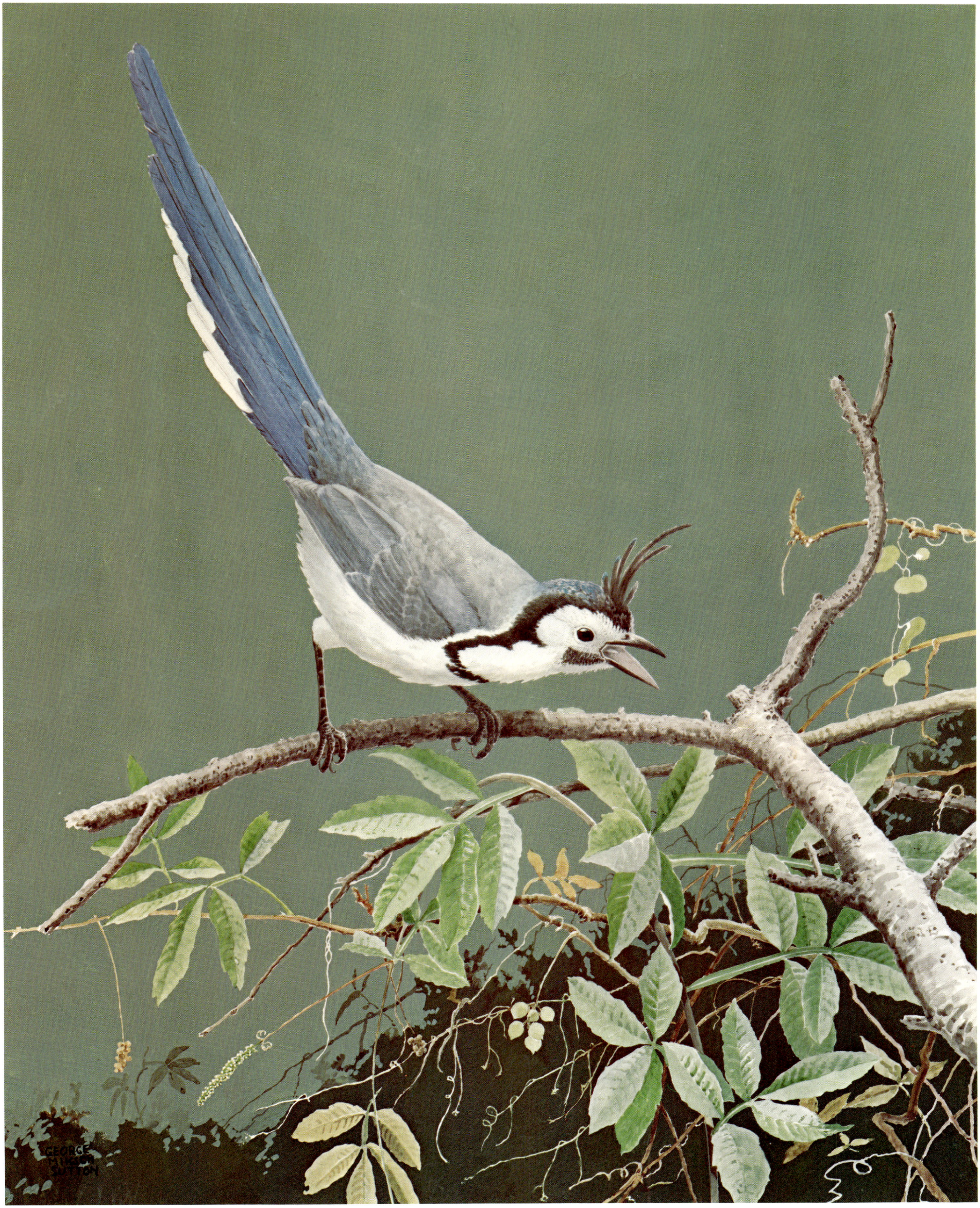
GEORGE
SUTTON

BROWN JAY

The Brown Jays *(Psilorhinus morio)* that inhabit the wooded lowlands of southern Tamaulipas pay little attention to the gentle, soft-spoken country folk, the *paisanos*, who move back and forth with their burros and mules along the trails; but let a man with a gun, especially one of those "gringos" from afar, try moving stealthily through the brush, and a Brown Jay is sure to notice him. The robust, crow-size bird slips up, silent as a shadow, inspects man and gun, expresses suspicion with an odd, barely audible popping sound, then, convinced that the situation bodes evil of some sort, it grips its perch tightly with strong toes, lowers its head, opens its beak wide, and hurls forth a ringing *pe-ah! pe-ah!* loud enough to send all timid creatures to cover, lure all curious creatures to the thicket's edge, and summon every Brown Jay of the neighborhood. Soon a dozen jays have gathered. Among the black-billed adults are young birds, each with black-and-yellow bill. "The enemy is here. He is moving!" the clamor declares. The gringo, annoyed but helpless, since shooting would frighten his quarry as well as the jays, stands perfectly still, wondering what to do. The outcry subsides, though the odd popping continues. The gringo takes a step forward and bedlam instantly resumes. "The enemy is moving again. He must be watched! Never for an instant is he to be unwatched!" the jays proclaim. The gringo, too intelligent to waste energy wishing that he could rub some lamp and become invisible, wonders whether he'd not be better off back at camp.

The Brown Jay's popping is not vocal. It is produced by the inflating—or possibly the deflating—of an odd little "furcular pouch" of skin on the chest, a spherical sac about the size of a big cherry that is sometimes barely visible when fully inflated but quite hidden by feathers when folded back. The *paisanos* call the bird the *papán*, in imitation of the sound (see Sutton and Gilbert, 1942, *Condor*, 44: 160-65). As stated above, the popping evinces curiosity or suspicion. It is not involuntary. The birds have their reasons for producing the sound. It is their way of telling each other that caution is advisable.

We saw Brown Jays close to the house at the Rancho Rinconada, especially early in the morning about the time we were getting up. At night the fog was often bad, so we only partly opened the doorlike shutters at the windows. The birds gathered when they heard us stirring. It required careful observation morning after morning to confirm our suspicion that they lined up on branches in such a way as to let each one look in. There they were, six or eight of them as a rule, probably a family group, one above the other, none obstructing the vision of any of its fellows, each popping as if having hiccups. The not very scientific thought crossed our minds that the popping might evince not only curiosity and suspicion but also something akin to guilty conscience. The birds should have known better than to look in at that particular time of day.

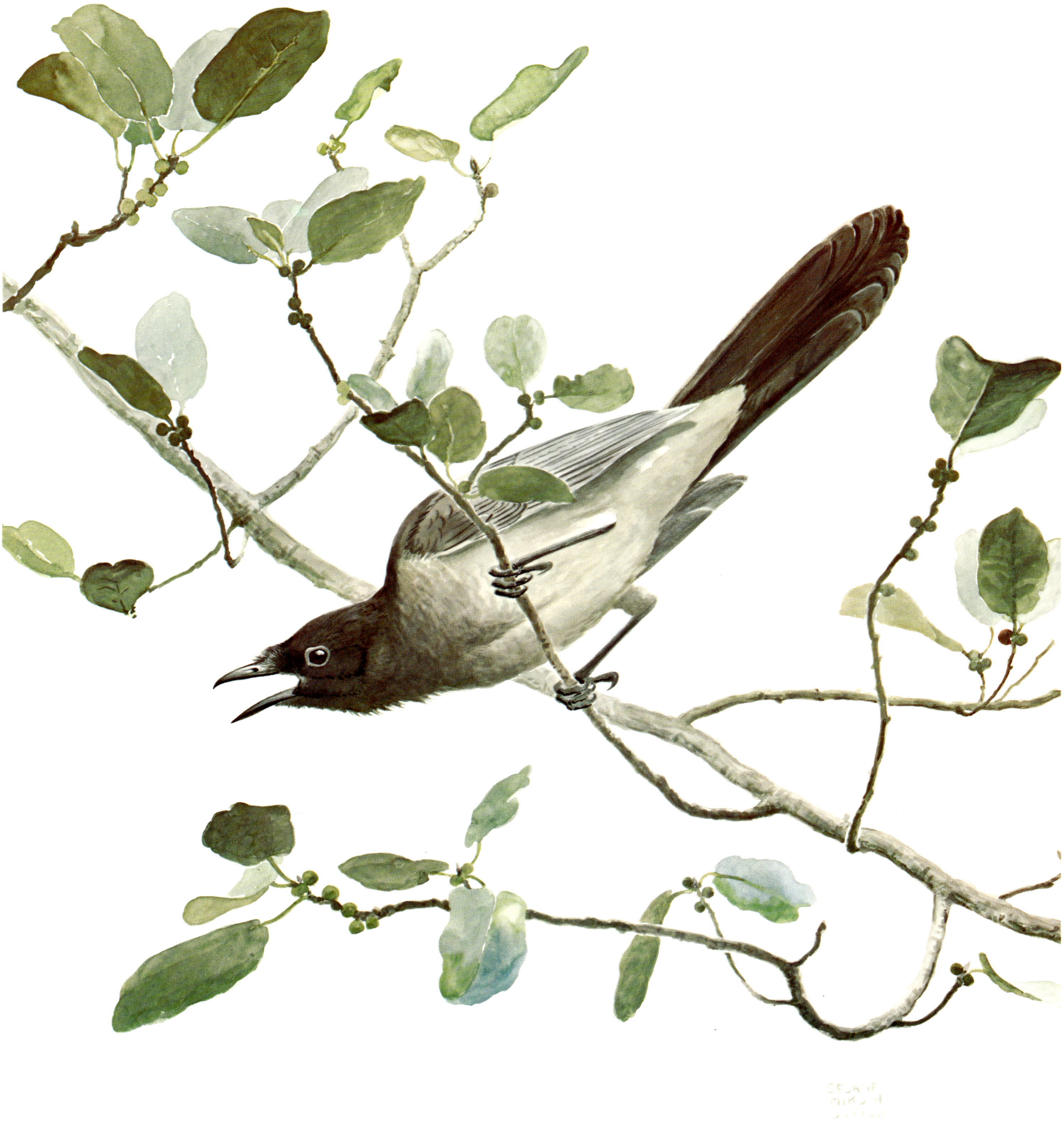

GREEN JAY

The geographical distribution of the Green Jay *(Cyanocorax yncas)*, a handsome species that certainly looks bright enough to be tropical, is puzzling. Though absent from most of Central America, it is found at low elevations from northern Venezuela southward through parts of Colombia and Ecuador to northern Bolivia and from northern Honduras northward to Yucatán and the mouth of the Río Grande and, on the west side of Mexico, to the State of Nayarit. Throughout most of this extensive range it is yellow-eyed; but in San Luis Potosí, Tamaulipas, and southern Texas it is brown-eyed. For years I was sorely puzzled by the brown eyes of birds I had seen and handled in the Lower Río Grande Valley, for the great bird artist, Louis Agassiz Fuertes, had depicted the species as yellow-eyed (see *Bird-Lore*, 1919, plate opp. p. 149). The explanation of the striking discrepancy was this: Fuertes had seen and handled yellow-eyed birds in South America and in Veracruz, but he had had little, if any, field experience within the range of the brown-eyed birds.

Except in the breeding season, when it becomes rather secretive, the Green Jay is noisy, gregarious, and noticeable. Moving about in small flocks, family groups perhaps, it announces its presence with harsh, rapidly repeated *cha-cha-cha* call notes. As the birds fly from thicket to thicket a certain amount of green and blue meets the eye of the observer, but the conspicuous feature of each bird is the light yellow at each side of the tail, patches of color that flash as the birds reduce speed and swoop upward just before alighting.

Green Jays' nests that I have seen were big, well built, and deeply cupped, but so thin-walled that I could see and even count the eggs without climbing above them for an unobstructed look. The highest nest I have seen was 12 feet above a sloping bank in a small tree. The eggs are grayish or bluish white, with a yellowish or olive tinge, marked with fairly thick brown and gray speckling that often forms a wreath around the larger end. The young hatch naked, in this respect resembling the well-known Blue Jay *(Cyanocitta cristata)*. The skin of the hatchlings is, appropriately enough, greenish gray.

According to my field notes, my party did not see the Green Jay at Jalapa, Veracruz, in 1939, but a male specimen collected by Ernest P. Edwards along the Río Atoyac four miles northwest of the town of Potrero, Veracruz, on April 12, 1947, had bright yellow eyes.

What do I remember most clearly about the Green Jay? Not the chatter of the little flocks as they romp through the thicket, not the apparent fearlessness of a mother bird brooding her three naked young, not the two birds that visited a certain vine for berries, as shown in my drawing—not any of these, but rather a single bird sound asleep in the very heart of a tangle of vines in the middle of the night. I was hunting owls with a flashlight. As I directed the bright rays through the thorny branches they suddenly illuminated what appeared to be a big, fluffy, light yellow ball, nothing more. I saw no head, for the bill was tucked into the plumage between the back and shoulders; no tail, for that part of the bird I simply could not see; no, just a fluffy ball of yellow that did not "come to" as I inspected it from a distance of perhaps ten feet; that stayed where it was, spherical, seemingly imperturbable, motionless save for the slight lifting and lowering of plumage that accompanied slow breathing—the only living adult Green Jay I've ever seen that was not fully awake and "up to something or other."

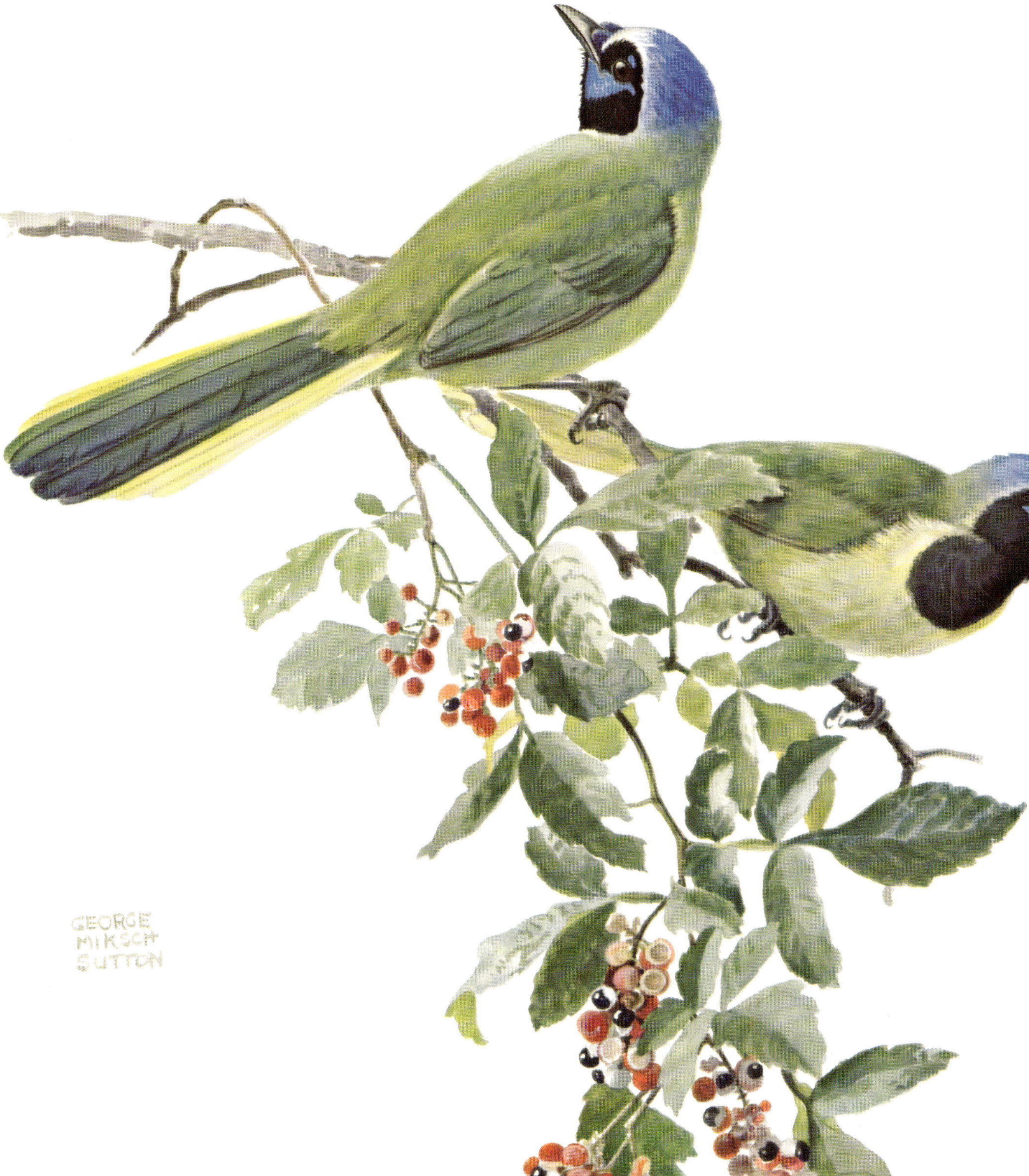
GEORGE
MIKSCH
SUTTON

GRAY-BARRED WREN

One of our camps in Michoacán was on a slope above Lake Pátzcuaro along the old, old cobblestone road leading to the mountain village of Tacámbaro. We were well situated there, for the birds of the pine forest were all about us, an extensive stand of mature oaks was only a hundred yards away, and there were cleared areas not much farther off in which the vegetation was strikingly different from that of either the pine woods or the oak woods. The oaks, alas, were being felled right and left for charcoal. The cleared areas were bright with flowers.

Not a single bird of the pine woods was really conspicuous. Occasionally we heard the husky song of a tanager far overhead or the plaintive calling of a trogon in the distance, but often the whole forest was strangely silent. The oak woods were noisier. There we often heard jays squawking. The most noticeable bird-sounds at camp were those of big wrens of a species I had never seen before. The wrens were responsible for what went down in my notes as "odd clacketty chatter"—not a bad description, really, except that it failed to convey the idea that two or more birds might be making the sounds at the same time. At first I thought that the chatter included an occasional "descending trill," but I never *saw* one of the wrens producing such a sound. The "chatter" was rough, raspy, not at all tuneful; when given in duet or chorus it was almost bizarre.

The best looks I had at the wrens were in the early morning, when the air was chilly. Then, fluffed up and perched well above ground where the sun would soon find them, they were sluggish. With the binocular I could see that they were grayish white, heavily barred and otherwise marked with dark gray. Nowhere in their plumage was there an extensive area either white or gray, and the only tinge of brown seemed to be on the flanks. Their eyes were light gray, not black or brown, like those of most passerine birds, but pale ashy gray.

The more I saw of these wrens the more remarkable they seemed. They went about not singly or in pairs, but in small companies. While foraging they explored the vegetation thoroughly, often hanging upside down from a twig, leaf, or root. They were especially fond of big airplants, which were not in full bloom. The "clacketty chatter" became doubly interesting when I learned that it was sometimes produced midair, while one bird was chasing another. I refused to believe that a chased bird deliberately slowed down to permit itself to be pecked, but often I saw the pursuer catching up and pecking at the tail and rump plumage of the other. Whether all this was "allopreening" or mere play was a question (see Elliott and Davis, 1965, *Condor*, 67: 352). At any rate, my nickname for the big wren was "rump-nipper." I was not at all sure of its correct "book name." According to one authority, the correct full name was Huitzilac Cactus Wren, but the first of those three words was meaningless, and the birds certainly were not frequenting cactus, so I was at a loss. Currently the species is known as the Gray-barred Wren (*Campylorhynchus megalopterus*).

My drawing, made on February 10, 1949, shows the wrens hunting for insects and spiders around one of the big airplants. The epiphyte was well above ground, so I had to cut it off and bring it down before drawing it. The tall spike of buds, not one of which was about to open, had a fine sculptured appearance that I greatly admired.

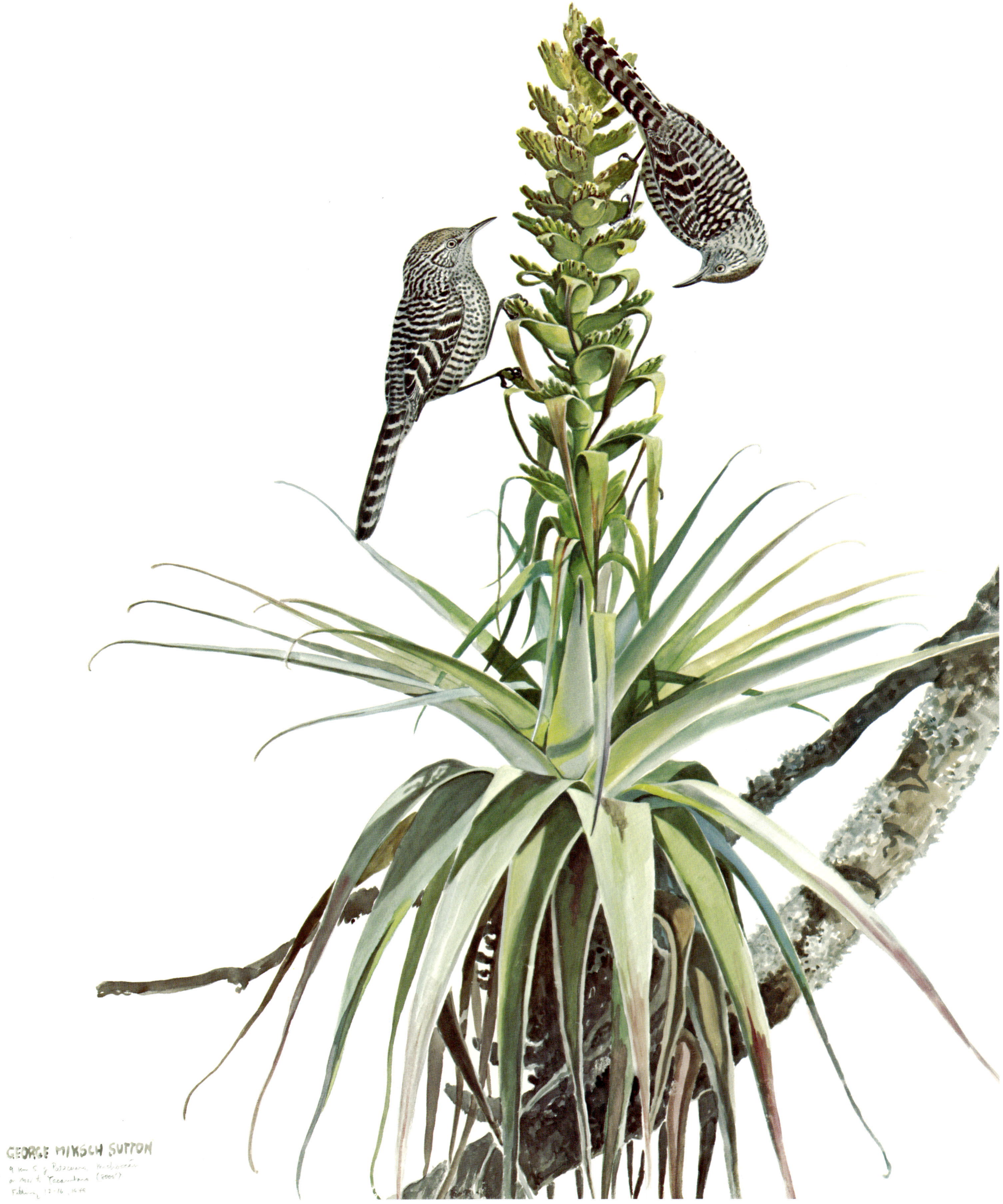
GEORGE MIKSCH SUTTON

GRAY SILKY

At our camp close to the old cobblestone road leading from Lake Pátzcuaro up to the village of Tacámbaro in Michoacán, I became acquainted with the Gray Silky *(Ptilogonys cinereus)*, an elegant member of the Ptilogonatidae, a New World family of four species sometimes called collectively the "silky-flycatchers." Each of the four is, I believe, expert enough at catching insects on the wing, but the Ptilogonatidae are not at all closely related to the New World flycatchers, the Tyrannidae, or the Old World flycatchers, the Muscicapidae, so calling them "flycatchers" of any sort is misleading. Currently taxonomists believe them to be close to the Bombycillidae, the waxwings, a disposition that strikes me as reasonable in view of the fact that all silkies and all waxwings are short-legged, small-billed, and exquisitely smooth of plumage—not to mention their fondness for berries.

Near camp in February of 1949 certain deciduous trees were so covered with mistletoe that they appeared to be quite green even though all their own leaves had dropped off the preceding fall. The mistletoe was of at least two kinds, one with small, spherical white berries (like those in my drawing), the other with much larger, elongate, purplish black, fluted berries. The silkies consumed the berries of both, and so dependent were the birds on this food that I could count on seeing them in certain heavily parasitized hawthorn trees at almost any time. The call note that announced arrival and departure was unmusical, composed of two or three syllables, and suggested to me the words *take a look*. Not often did I hear this note while the birds were eating. The males were more brightly colored and more noticeably crested than the females. On one occasion I heard what might have been a bit of true song from a single bird as it flew over.

The silkies went about in small flocks as a rule, not in pairs, for the breeding season had not yet started. I have never seen a Gray Silky's nest, though a former student of mine, Frederick W. Loetscher Jr., found a nest 40 feet up in an "unclimbable" tree near Jalapa, Veracruz, on May 1, 1939, and Robert J. Newman has well described a nest that he found four miles west of the village of Acultzingo, Veracruz, not far from the Puebla state line. This nest, which was 30 feet up in a crotch on a "steeply slanted" slender branch in the "dense upper foliage of a 35-foot oak," and which held two newly hatched young on May 24, 1949, was "a work of exquisite artistry." Its exterior was "completely shingled with large pieces of foliose lichen, whose crinkled surfaces create a variegated pattern of blackish browns and frosty greenish gray" (Newman, 1950, *Condor*, 52: 157).

In Colima we saw very few Gray Silkies near the Hacienda el Cóbano in January of 1971. We had excellent looks at one bird that measured handsomely up to expectations when it fell to eating mistletoe berries right in front of us. In May of 1974, however, we did not see the species anywhere near the hacienda. At that season it was at higher elevations. On a wooded slope in Jalisco, at about 6,500 feet, it was considerably the commonest bird that we saw on May 21. There, many of them continued to fly out from high in the pines, catching insects midair. I hadn't before realized how clearly the white in the widespread tail would show from below. How tiny the birds looked, a hundred feet or so overhead!

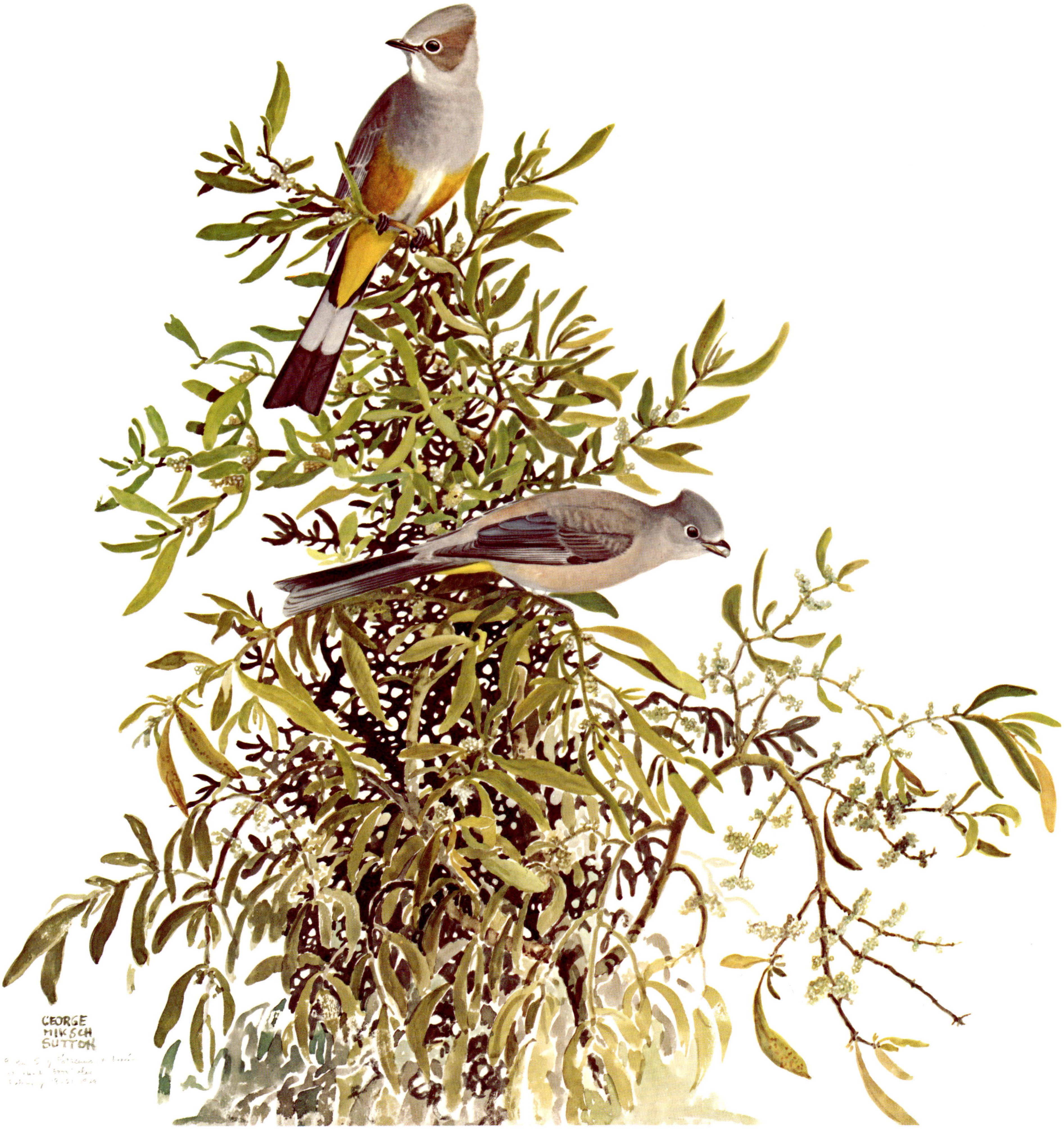
GEORGE
MIKSCH
SUTTON

PEPPERSHRIKE

Seeing a new bird is always exciting, especially if the observer has a really good look at it, and even more especially if he can thumb through a field guide on the spot and ascertain just what it is. The guide doesn't always help, for there are "look alikes" among birds the world over. These "look alikes" can be fun, annoyance, even a kind of anguish, all at the same time.

My first *living* Peppershrike *(Cyclarhis gujanensis)* was no problem, no problem at all. I was in brushland north of Tamazunchale, San Luis Potosí, well away from the Río Moctezuma and the big trees lining its bank. The April morning was bright with color and sound. Suddenly, in a thorny shrub at eye-level only a few yards away, appeared a chunky little yellow-breasted bird that I had never before seen in Mexico, that our party had not listed that season, that I had never, in fact, seen *alive* anywhere. But it was not new. I recognized it at once. Its heavy bill, the rufous and gray of its head, the olive green of its back, wings, and tail—all were familiar. Its shape and the colors of its plumage did not puzzle me in the least, but its way of climbing about, the brick-red of its eyes, and its lovely, full-throated song had me fairly gasping in surprise.

Why had the bird been so instantly identifiable? Because years before, at the Carnegie Museum in Pittsburgh, while I was an assistant on the staff there, a distinguished ornithologist from afar had asked me to show her the museum's "series of *Cyclarhis* specimens," and I, alas, had to be told what a *Cyclarhis* was. That was long before I had given a "Birds of the World" course anywhere; but even if the visitor had asked to see the museum's "peppershrikes" I'd have been bewildered. So, under circumstances of that sort, once I learned what a *Cyclarhis* and a peppershrike were, I could not forget. On that long-ago occasion in Pittsburgh, with literally dozens of specimens spread out before us, I had learned that *Cyclarhis gujanensis* ranged from northeastern Mexico southward through Central America and northern South America to Peru, Brazil, and northern Argentina.

In the spring of 1941, along the Río Sabinas in southwestern Tamaulipas, I was to see the living Peppershrike again, this time at the northernmost tip of its range. On March 19 of that year I painted it, using as a perch for the bird figure the very shrub I had seen it climbing about in. There I heard again, over and over, the species' loud, clearly enunciated, remarkably mellow song. So securely did the phrases fasten themselves in my mind that years later, when I heard them while peering down into the sacred well at Chichén-Itzá, Yucatán, I recognized them immediately. Even more recently, while I was on a cruise up the Amazon, the only well-defined bird song that our party heard at one point as we were walking upslope from the water's edge was that of a Peppershrike. At first I didn't quite trust myself, for we were in a part of the world that was bewilderingly new to me, but the longer I listened the more confident I became. How those rhythmic, well-turned phrases carried me back to enchanted hours in Mexico!

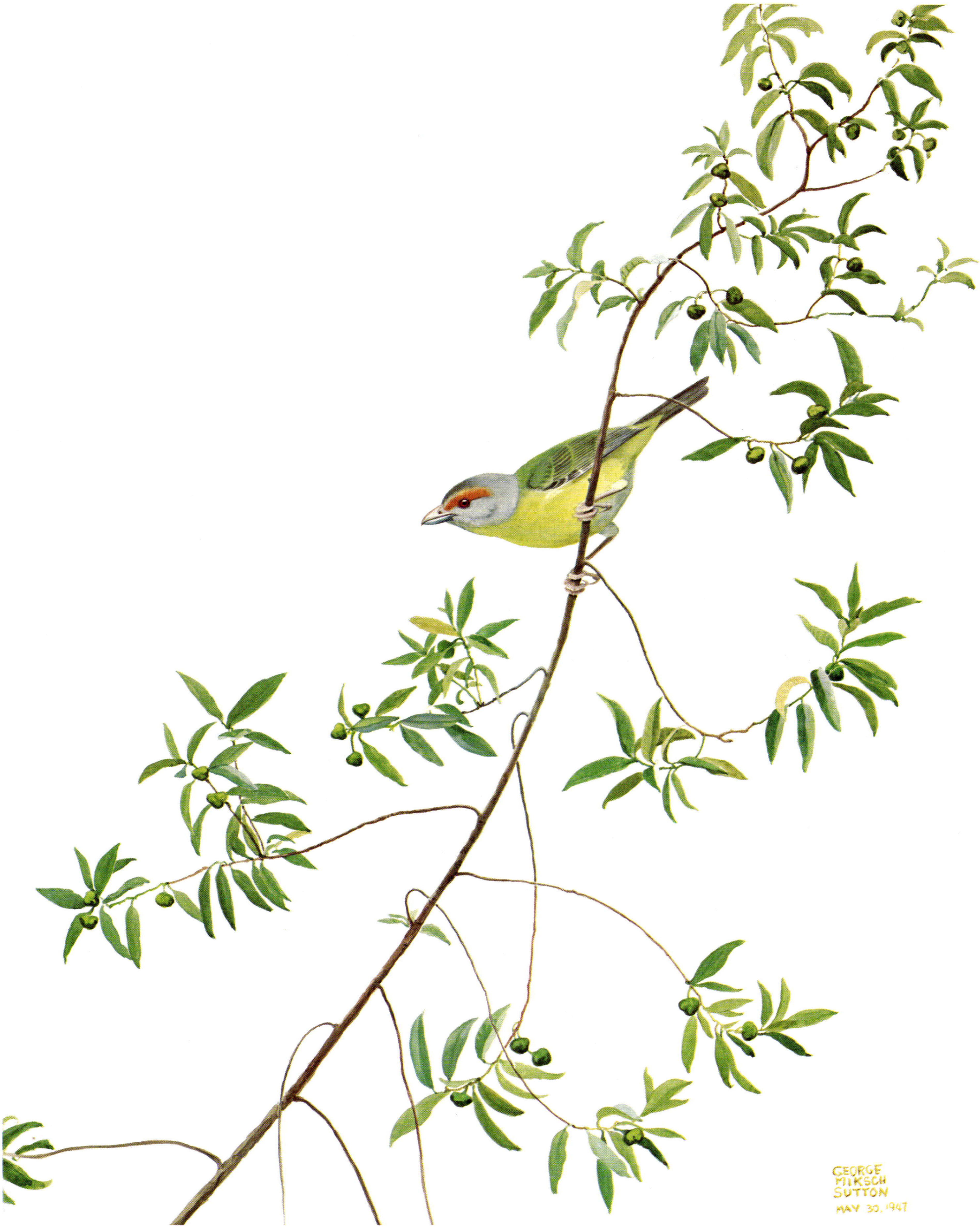
GEORGE
MIKSCH
SUTTON
MAY 30, 1947

CHESTNUT-SIDED SHRIKE-VIREO

Not often nowadays do I allow myself to make a drawing of a bird I do not know well. Some years ago I found myself bound by contract to do a series of drawings representing every bird family known. By the time I had finished that series I said to myself, "Never again." I had copied photographs, corresponded far and wide, and depended on imagination when all else failed, winding up with the miserable feeling that I had borrowed, plagiarized, even lied. But when, on May 24, 1973, we captured in a mist-net the first living Chestnut-sided Shrike-Vireo *(Vireolanius melitophrys)* I had ever seen, I knew that I'd have to paint it.

The little bird's most conspicuous features were, to my way of thinking, its ever so slightly silvery yellowish-white eyes and its strong, flesh-colored tarsi and toes. It was obviously sturdy. There was nothing delicate about the way in which those toes gripped my fingers. I made no attempt to see whether it could bite, for its bill was heavy and slightly hooked. I could not help wondering whether shrike-vireos ever impale their prey on thorns, as shrikes do. The sharp-eyed bird in my hand looked perfectly capable of dispatching big insects, centipedes, possibly even tarantulas and very small lizards.

The group attending the seminar at the Hacienda el Cóbano had traveled that day to a volcano in Jalisco. Everyone had piled into two big buses, and the buses had climbed, climbed, climbed, finally to a sort of shelf below the crater at an elevation of about 6,500 feet. The road had been tortuous and at times difficult. Considerable stretches of it had been paved, long since, with cobblestones. On our way up we had passed tiny farmyards complete with sheds, cribs, chickens, and "animals," wonderfully self-sufficient little "socio-economic entities" clinging precariously to the slopes, miles from the nearest village, but oddly homey-looking. As we passed these tiny farmsteads, I could not help wondering whether anyone there ever sent or received one piece of mail during the course of a whole year.

At the shelf where the two buses were parked there was an official station of some sort. A trifle short of breath as a result of the altitude, we found ourselves among tall pines, beneath which not much vegetation aside from grass grew. Steep-sided deep ravines leading down from the road were covered by a tangle of shrubbery and vines that looked impenetrable. I tried one descent—in pursuit of a puzzling bird-call—and decided to stay on the road. So steep were some of those slopes that if a man were to lose his footing he might fall, quite literally fall, a long way, unless the webbing of vines proved strong enough to catch and hold him.

The bird we saw most frequently that day was the Gray Silky *(Ptilogonys cinereus)*, a species I had painted in 1949 in the State of Michoacán. A surprise of the trip was a Blue Mockingbird *(Melanotis caerulescens)* at an elevation far above what I thought the upper limit of the species' distribution might be.

Getting plants that would serve as models for my shrike-vireo drawing back to the hacienda where I had paints and drawing-board proved to be difficult. We wrapped the bases of the twigs with wetted paper napkins, thus keeping the leaves fresh, but the black berries fell off one by one, despite careful handling. The pretty bed-straw toward the bottom of the picture is, so far as I can see, exactly the same species that grows in my back yard in Norman, Oklahoma!

GEORGE
MIKSCH
SUTTON

TROPICAL PARULA WARBLER

On his first visit to a tropical part of Mexico a bird student from the United States may be truly bewildered by what he sees and hears. The vegetation around him has a profligacy that is almost frightening. Against the deep green of the foliage flash patches of bright color, as unfamiliar birds fly past. From the shadowy woods come strange calls, some of them so clearly enunciated as to remind him instantly of certain pronounceable syllables, words, or phrases. So humiliated is he by his ignorance that when some bird that he *does* know presents itself, he is more bewildered then ever. "Why that bird looks exactly like a so-and-so," he says to himself, "but of course it can't be that. Look where I am!"

What does he know and what *not know*! He hears a thin wispy song far above him, perceives that the singer is little and active, that its throat and breast are yellow, and that it has two white wing-bars. A warbler, of course. The bird drops from its twig, snatches an insect as it descends, and alights only a few yards from him. The yellow of the throat and breast has a rich, burnt-orange tinge. There is no white at all about the eyes. The bird can be nothing but a Tropical Parula *(Parula pitiayumi)*, a warbler found from the Lower Río Grande Valley southward to Bolivia, Paraguay, and northern Argentina. It looks much like the Northern Parula *(P. americana)*, except that it has no white at all about its eye and no hint of dark band across its chest.

I have seen the Tropical Parula in many parts of Mexico and have paid much attention to its singing. At Linares, Nuevo León, on March 4, 1941, I listened to a bird that sang two very different songs, one much like the characteristic *zeeeee-zip* of the Northern Parula, the other a *jeery, jeery, jeery, zeee* that reminded me of songs of the Cerulean Warbler *(Dendroica cerulea)* that I had heard in West Virginia. I believe the two songs are equally characteristic at the height of the pairing season. Males that we saw in Colima in January of 1971 were not singing.

My painting was made along the Río Sabinas in southwestern Tamaulipas on May 23, 1947. I drew the bird from a freshly-collected specimen before even trying to envision the final picture; then with easel and other equipment in tow, I walked along one of the river-level trails until I found a blooming orchid plant low enough for direct-from-life delineation. As I worked there, hour after hour, I was surprised by the several birds that came, one by one, to the thicket's edge, each of them curious about a man who "stayed put" so long. Among the investigators was a big, handsome, rufous-and-gray squirrel that came very close, giving the impression, as he sniffed in my direction, that he could not see me very well.

Four days later, in a cypress near the river, I saw a female Tropical Parula carrying a small green caterpillar in her bill. This was proof enough that young birds were being fed, but I did not find either them or the nest.

GEORGE MIKSCH SUTTON

FAN-TAILED WARBLER

One of the well-named birds of Mexico is the Fan-tailed Warbler *(Euthlypis lachrymosa)*, a large warbler (5½ inches) found from southern Sonora, southern Chihuahua, and southwestern Tamaulipas southward on both Pacific and Atlantic coastal slopes as far as northwestern Nicaragua. I say well-named, for I believe I have never seen a Fan-tailed Warbler with its tail anything but spread. The tail is showy, too, for every one of the twelve feathers is clearly tipped with white. Since the species' habitat is shady, the white of the tail-tip probably helps the birds to keep track of one another.

We saw very little of the Fan-tailed Warbler in southwestern Tamaulipas in early March of 1938. That year we neither saw nor heard it along the Río Sabinas, though we did obtain two specimens on the wooded foothill well above river-level. In 1939 we did not see it anywhere in Tamaulipas, though I did find two pairs along a wooded ravine not far south of Tamazunchale, San Luis Potosí. In 1941 we saw it for the first time close to the Río Sabinas; during that visit we learned its song, a bright performance of several syllables, only the last of which usually reached the ear. According to my notes, the last syllable invariably had a downward inflection, making it all sound something like *titchy, titchy, beecher*. I heard this song many times in 1941 and again on May 15, 1947. On that date, while climbing the steep slope near the lovely waterfall at El Salto, San Luis Potosí, every member of our party heard the song repeatedly, though we did not often see the singers.

In January of 1949, while camped at Paño Ayuctle along the Río Sabinas, we were surprised to find Fan-tailed Warblers common at river-level. We did not see them often, but on three occasions we caught one in a mist-net, and on January 21 and 22 closely observed two birds, probably a pair, in a shadowy tangle near the mouth of one of the river's little tributaries. Here I could watch the handsome birds to my heart's content. I was surprised to learn that they walked, rather than hopped, when on the ground. Here, on January 23, with a netted specimen and the two uncaptured birds as models, I made my picture.

When I started the drawing I was comforted by realizing that the philodendron plant with its big leaves and elusive highlights would "stay put"; but I didn't expect to see much of the warblers. Imagine my surprise when I found that the little birds stayed close by, that they gradually came closer, that eventually they were moving quietly about almost under—actually within inches of—the easel's three legs, so close that I could see every detail. I found it hard to tell myself that the affection I felt for the pair was not returned in kind. Fond of them I was, for they were so co-operative. When I noticed that they were snatching mosquitoes from the air I decided that they were among the nicest little birds I had ever known. They did not, alas, catch every mosquito.

On March 19, 1949, not far from the very spot at which I had made my drawing, I saw several Fan-tailed Warblers among the birds that moved through the brush just ahead of an advancing ant army.

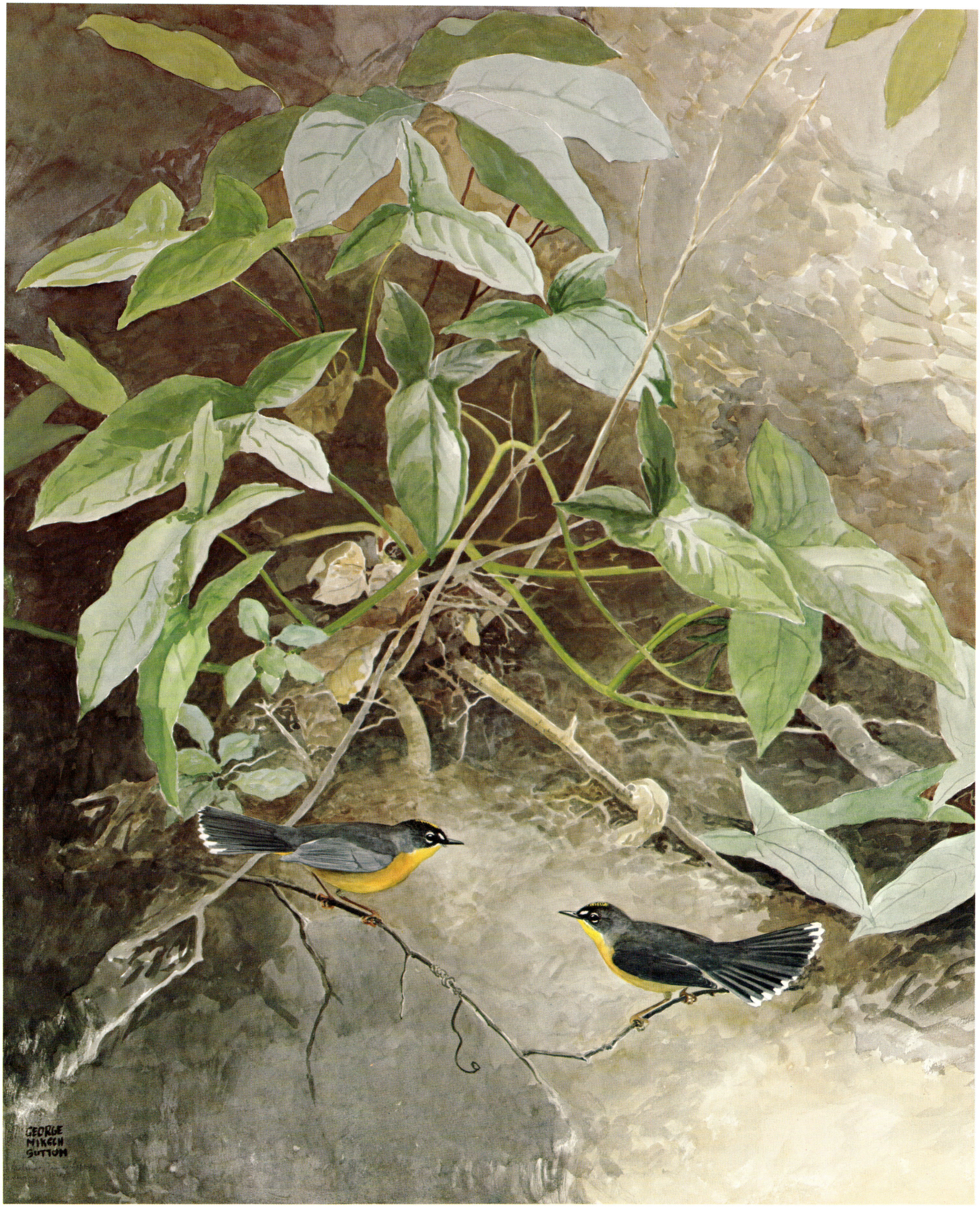
GEORGE
MIKSCH
SUTTON

HOODED ORIOLE

Among the most brightly colored of Mexico's songbirds is the little Hooded Oriole *(Icterus cucullatus)*, a species that ranges northward into the southern United States from the Lower Río Grande Valley in Texas westward to California. When I visited Mexico in 1938 and 1939 I did not see the bird often, but when Sewall Pettingill, Bob Lea, Dwain Warner, and I established ourselves for a season's work at the Rancho Rinconada in southwestern Tamaulipas in mid-March, 1941, we saw it daily. Indeed, a male bird that sang from the topmost pad of a prickly-pear cactus fence within a few feet of our kitchen window was our closest neighbor for weeks. When not singing, he sipped nectar from small pink blossoms that studded every twig of a tree in the yard. Occasionally he ate an insect that also had been attracted by the flowers. If moved to sing, he usually returned to his cactus fence. When we nailed two halves of an orange to a branch he soon found them, claimed them for his very own, and defended them stoutly against other birds—especially a male Alta Mira Oriole about twice as heavy as he.

The Hooded Oriole's mate, whose sharp *weet* call note we heard from occasionally, visited the little pink blossoms from time to time, though by herself. On April 1 we watched her stripping fibers from the edge of a palmetto leaf and carrying these to a partly built nest. For five days she worked. The male did not help her, though his fervent singing probably encouraged her. The nest, a neat cup rather than a deep pouch, was sewn securely to the under side of one of the great palmetto fans. There nest and eggs might be tossed about by the wind, but rain would not reach them.

Sewall Pettingill will never forget another female Hooded Oriole who decided that his burlap blind had been erected especially for her. The blind was on a platform not far from the big monkey's-ear tree in which there were the beginnings of an Alta Mira Oriole's nest. Pettingill was bent on recording the various stages in the construction of that conspicuous nest. As he worked, day after day, he noticed that a female Hooded Oriole was coming and going, actually entering his blind but apparently paying no attention to him. He thought that the little bird was after flies or spiders. Then, to his surprise, he found the neat, tightly sewn beginnings of a nest a few inches above his head. Trying to convince the oriole that she should find another nest-site, he closed with safety pins the opening in the burlap for his camera's lens. But did the oriole get the message? She did not. She forced her way past lens and safety pins, dragging in strips of palmetto fiber two feet long, and went ahead with her weaving. Our comment at meals was that she should have used some of Pettingill's hair.

A Hooded Oriole nest that I found on June 3, 1947, at Linares, Nuevo León, was about 15 feet up on the under side of a palmetto fan. In the nest were two oriole eggs, each white, marked with delicate black scrawls, and two slightly larger eggs of the Red-eyed Cowbird *(Tangavius aeneus)*. These were immaculate, one white, the other very pale blue. The shell of the white one had been scratched so badly that I could not help feeling that some bird (perhaps the oriole, perhaps another female cowbird than the one who had laid it) had tried to remove it from the nest. This feeling was confirmed when I found another white cowbird egg, unbroken but much scratched, in the grass under the tree.

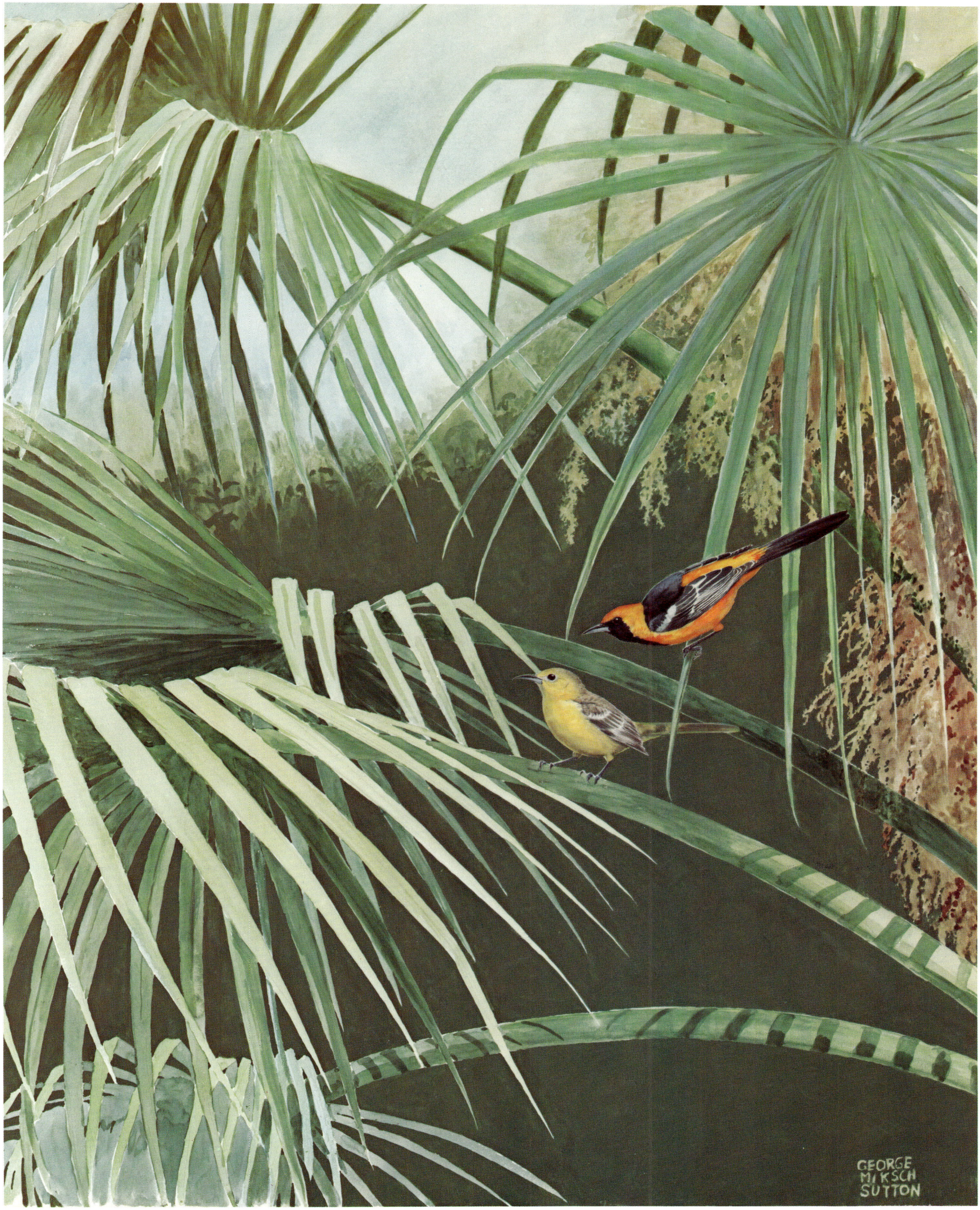
GEORGE
MIKSCH
SUTTON

ALTA MIRA ORIOLE

Observant persons who travel the Laredo–Mexico City highway are likely to be puzzled by oriole nests up to 2 feet long hanging in plain sight from branches of dead trees and telephone wires. Well constructed and durable, the nests hang there until rain and wind wear them out. Even an old, long-since abandoned nest may look fairly new, but the curious person who hopes to see a bird going to it may wait in vain. The oriole that builds these nests is the handsome Alta Mira Oriole or Black-throated Oriole *(Icterus gularis)*. In eastern Mexico the species ranges northward to the Lower Río Grande Valley. I have seen much of it in Tamaulipas at Ciudad Victoria and along the Río Sabinas near the hill village of Gómez Farías and in San Luis Potosí at Valles and Tamazunchale. Whether it ranges as far northward as Colima in western Mexico remains to be ascertained; I thought I saw it there in January, 1971. Among orioles that I know well, it is unique in one important way: the colors of the female cannot be described as dull or "protective"; furthermore, she sings.

Though at a loss to explain just why the bird should do so, I am convinced that the Alta Mira Oriole advertises its nest. My friend Sewall Pettingill, observing from a blind the behavior of a singing bird and the nest it was building, came to realize that it was doing all the work by itself; that no other bird accompanied it as it flew back and forth; that for days it continued to sing while working, not as if soliloquizing, but in loud, clear phrases that could be heard a long way off; that it might, indeed, be announcing that it wanted a mate. It was so brightly colored that Pettingill and I both thought that it was a male. The photographic record is extremely interesting. The bird started building toward the end of a drooping branch about 35 feet up in a fairly large ear-tree *(Enterolobium cyclocarpum)*. A few days later it deserted the barely-started structure and began a new one on another branch of the same tree. The new nest was started on April 7 and finished, lining and all, 18 to 26 days later. On April 22 (but not before then), Pettingill saw what must have been the newly-arrived mate, a bird that was not noticeably brighter than the builder (Sutton and Pettingill, 1954, *Condor*, 45: 125–32).

Who can say that most female Alta Mira orioles build their nests before finding a mate? Who can say that the females, rather than the males, lay claim to and defend nest territories? Whatever the answer to questions of this sort, these facts influence my thinking: of the many Alta Mira Oriole nests I have seen, not one was tucked away in an obscure place; in a series of adult Alta Mira Oriole specimens before me, one female is as bright as the brightest male and several males are as dull as the dullest female; the female Alta Mira Oriole sings brilliantly. In any event, nests are placed where they can easily be seen by other orioles and where predators will surely expose themselves if they attempt to crawl out the supporting branch or wire. Since nests are not hidden, their builders need not be protectively colored. We accept gladly enough the fact that Alta Mira Oriole nests are easy to find; but consider the audacity of that first female bird who decided that she'd attach her nest to a telephone wire!

I have yet to learn one important thing about the Alta Mira oriole's biology: the extent to which the species is parasitized by the Red-eyed Cowbird *(Tangavius aeneus)*. My guess is that the nest's narrowness at the top and deepness may discourage many a female cowbird, especially if other host species with more open nests are numerous. The Red-eyed Cowbird is a common species throughout a wide range. Its social parasitism has obviously helped it to achieve success. The Alta Mira Oriole may well be among its hosts.

My drawing is of a male bird perched on a spray of purple-wreath, a climbing shrub of the genus *Petrea* that is fairly common along the Sabinas. The pale parts of the drooping panicle are sepals, not petals. The fully opened corollas drop off when a bird alights near them, shaking its perch, but the sepals remain.

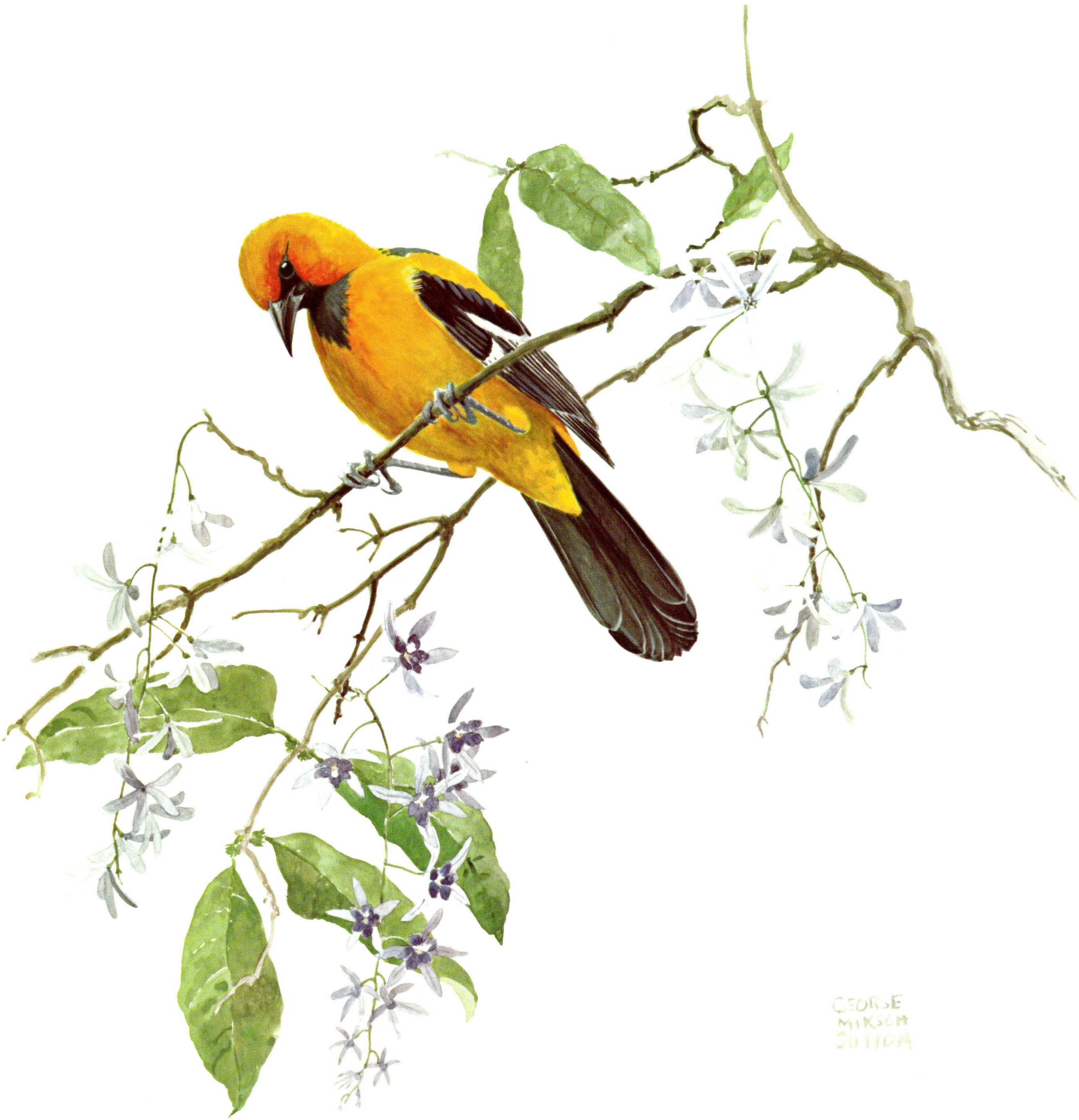
GEORGE
MIKSCH
SUTTON

BLACK-HEADED ORIOLE

Along a small stream north of Monterrey, Nuevo León, on a cool day in early February, 1938, I was completely fooled by whistles that I thought were those of a small boy on his way to a favorite fishing hole. So convinced was I that the whistles were human that I tried to get away from them, for I did not want to shoot specimens near anyone. The whistles—pleasing enough to the ear, but a bit "off key," without definite pattern, and therefore tuneless—were from a handsome black, white, and lemon-yellow bird, the Black-headed Oriole *(Icterus graduacauda)*. The species ranges from northwestern Guatemala northward to the State of Nayarit in the west and to Tamaulipas and Nuevo León in the east. The northern limits of its range are in southern Texas where, until recently, it was known as the Audubon's Oriole.

In southwestern Tamaulipas in 1941 we saw the Black-headed Oriole daily from March 14 to May 1. From the first of our stay to April 3 it went about in little flocks as a rule, often with birds of other small and middle-sized species, but from April 4 on, we saw it in pairs, and on April 19 I found a partly-finished nest about 15 feet up on a horizontal branch in a wild lime tree above a narrow trail through the thicket. The bird that was building this nest did not lead me to it. For a while I wondered whether it was a nest at all. I hid myself close by and waited. Presently a female oriole came to the nest with a long fiber in her bill and worked diligently for ten minutes or so. The nest was a shallow basket suspended from twigs and leaves, but unlike any oriole nest I had ever seen, it was not in the least pouchlike. Following its builder about, I watched her strip fibers from the edges of palmetto fans. So far as I could see, no mate accompanied her. I was not even sure that a male bird was singing in the vicinity. When two Brown Jays came by, the female oriole, quite by herself, gave chase—and fierce the chase was. Her cries of protest, of the same sort that she occasionally directed at me, were short and harsh, and their meaning was clear.

I visited the partly-finished nest repeatedly. On April 23 it was obviously far from completion, for I could see right through it. When the bird worked on it, she worked hard, but on several occasions when I visited it, I neither saw nor heard her or her mate in the immediate vicinity.

On the Mesa de Chipinque, that charming shelf on the mountain above Monterrey, on May 7, 1941, my friend Sewall Pettingill found a Black-headed Oriole's nest containing well-grown young. The nest was on a pine bough, of all places, suspended between two big cones.

My drawing is of a male perched on the petiole of a big philodendron leaf. I made the drawing on May 22, 1947. On our way back to the States that year we had an informal showing of my drawings in a small park near the courthouse in Lubbock, Texas. I made no point of displaying myself as the artist, being content with listening to comments. On seeing the Black-headed Oriole drawing one healthy looking citizen, probably a cattleman, said in a clear voice to a companion: "Man, wouldn't *that one* make grand wallpaper!" This statement was quoted to me often as our party traveled northward.

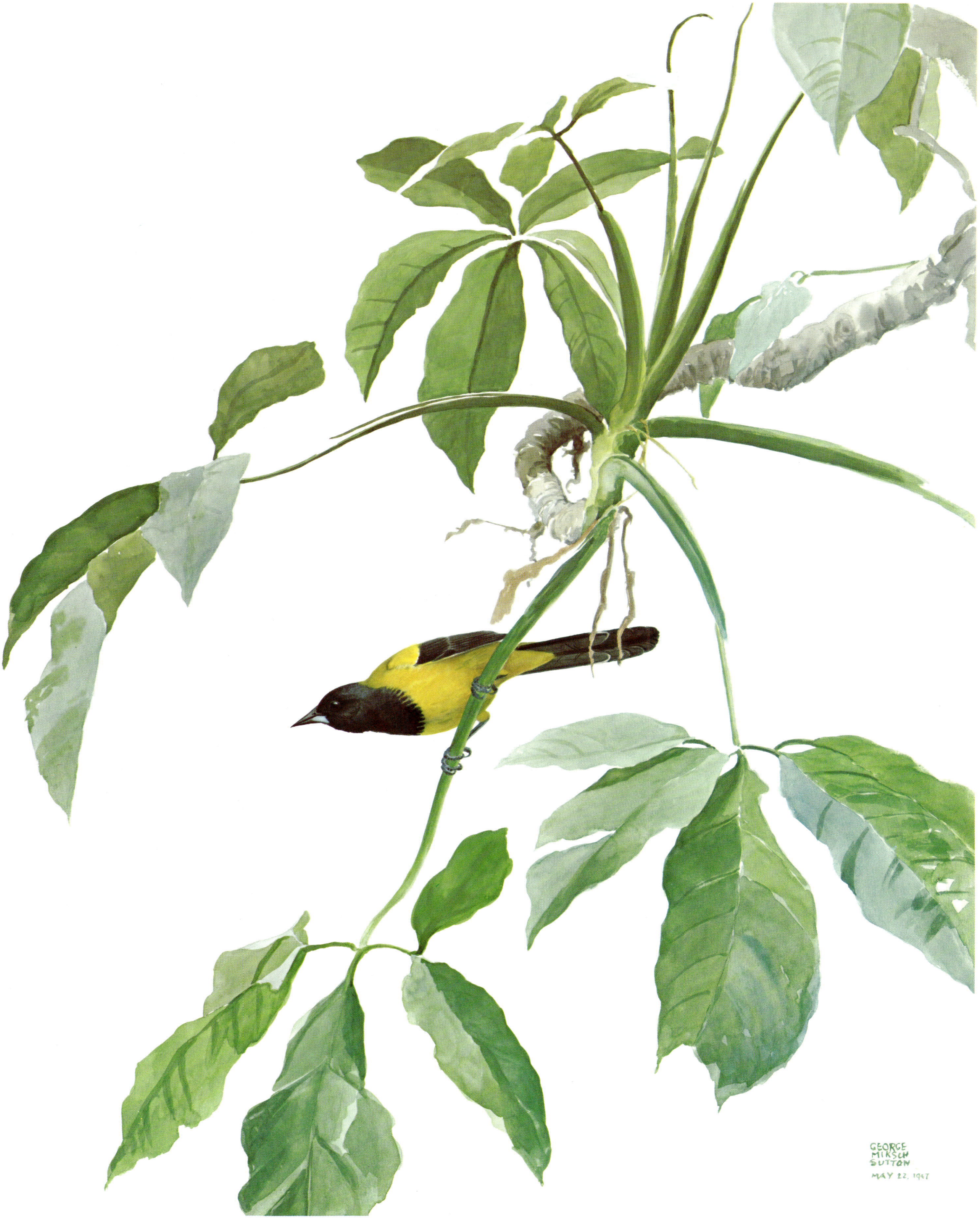
GEORGE
MIKSCH
SUTTON
MAY 22, 1947

ABEILLE'S ORIOLE

One of our most exciting camps in Michoacán in the early spring of 1949 was at about 10,000 feet elevation half way between Lake Pátzcuaro and the village of Tacámbaro. There we parked the truck at the edge of a grassy flat not far from a tiny farm at which we obtained for the pot a vegetable called the *patata*, a root that tasted, when cooked, not nearly as much like a potato as the spelling suggested. Among the "new" birds that we found there was the Abeille's or Black-backed Oriole *(Icterus abeillei)*, a bird now thought by some taxonomists to be conspecific with the Baltimore Oriole *(I. galbula)* and Bullock's Oriole *(I. bullockii)* of the United States. Though I am opposed to this "lumping" of the three forms, I must admit that the scolding call notes of Abeille's Orioles that lived near camp were very much like those of Baltimore Orioles that I had heard at Bethany, West Virginia, and Ithaca, New York, and of Bullock's Orioles that I had heard in far western Oklahoma. As for *songs* of the Abeille's, I have no comment, for I am not sure that I have heard that species' full song. The fact is worth recording, for the early fall songs of Baltimore Orioles that I have heard during the brief period between the birds' completion of the postnuptial molt and their departure for the south have been full-throated and tuneful, and I suspect that they sing often in winter.

The Abeille's Orioles visited deciduous trees near camp, but I saw them also in tall firs. They went about in flocks of four to ten birds, most of them females or young birds in a female-like plumage. They had a jaylike habit of hammering at their feet with their sharply pointed bills. This I interpreted as a pounding-open of seeds or cocoons until I discovered that their toes were often sticky with pitch—presumably from the fir trees. In any case, I have never seen a Baltimore or Bullock's Oriole pounding at its toes (or at food held in the toes) in any such manner.

Not for some time did I see a fully adult male Abeille's Oriole with black back and sides. The flocks squeaked up readily, behavior that did not surprise me, since I had often lured Baltimore and Bullock's Orioles down from the treetops with sounds of that sort.

The Abeille's were especially fond of a patch of giant thistles and scarlet-flowered, woolly-stemmed salvia growing on a slope about half a mile from camp. Here the birds may have spent the night, for I saw them there early in the morning, long before the sun had warmed the hummingbirds up enough to set their tiny wings to whirring. So much time did the orioles spend among the thistles that I decided to draw an adult male near the top of one; so, taking stool and drawing-board to a ledge at thistle-top level, I proceeded to draw the plant direct from life. This did not work out very well, partly because the ledge was narrow and partly because there were so many stems and flowers in front of me that I found it difficult to focus on any one plant. So I dug one thistle up, took it back to the truck, measured it (20 feet and almost 6 inches), cut the top 3 or 4 feet off, placed this in a bucket of water, and went ahead with the drawing.

Roger Hurd took a photograph of me with the towering thistle standing straight up at my side. Looking at the picture today gives me the feeling that I'm not very tall.

GEORGE
MIKSCH
SUTTON

SCRUB EUPHONIA

Euphonias are small-billed, short-tailed, finchlike little birds whose songs and call notes strike me as being almost anything but euphonious. Cynicism aside, the several species of the genus *Euphonia* are currently placed in the tanager family. The five that inhabit Mexico are 3½ to 5 inches long. Two of these range northward as far as Tamaulipas in the east and Sonora in the west, but nowhere quite into the United States. I have seen a good deal of three species, the lovely Blue-hooded Euphonia *(Euphonia elegantissima)*, the Yellow-throated Euphonia *(E. hirundinacea)*, and the little Scrub Euphonia *(E. affinis)*, the one shown in my drawing.

The name "scrub" is singularly unfortunate, for it seems to connote soapsuds on a floor, a rough-textured washcloth designed to make the face shine, or a nondescript athletic team. It refers, of course, to the "scrub" woodland the handsome little bird is supposed to inhabit; even so, it is ugly and not quite fair, even to the habitat. Those lovely woods along the Río Sabinas, the trees in which I saw *Euphonia affinis* every day, may not have been majestic—they may not have been for me a "forest primeval"—but they were not scrubby. The scrubby woods of the area were east of the Rancho Rinconada, out on the comparatively dry coastal plain. In those woods I did not even see *Euphonia affinis*.

An important fact about euphonias merits discussion. The little birds are confirmed eaters of mistletoe berries. So fond are they of this particular food that their lives consist largely of moving from clump to clump of mistletoe from morning to night. They may have special feeding periods, as many birds do, but I never witnessed such periods and I suspect that what appeared to be virtually incessant eating might have been correlated with the low caloric content of the berries or with the important fact that the berries pass through the birds' alimentary tracts without being thoroughly digested. In each berry is a seed enclosed in a fairly thick, sticky capsule. The berries, swallowed whole, pass out of the body devoid of skin and juice, but not of encapsulated seed. The droppings fall, some to the ground but some to twigs where, because of their viscosity, they cling to the bark. Here they dry. When rains fall the seeds germinate, and new mistletoe plants start. Thus do the euphonias, following time-honored procedure, assure themselves of a continuing food supply. The whole routine is good for all concerned, for despite the fact that the mistletoe, a true parasite, lives on the sap of the trees to which it clings, it never seems to harm them. As a rule the little birds defecate as they eat and just as they fly from the tree, so some of the precious droppings are almost sure to fall on twigs (see Sutton, 1951, *Wilson Bulletin*, 63: 235–37 and frontispiece showing Blue-hooded Euphonias).

The commonest mistletoe of the Sabinas Valley had orange berries, as shown in my drawing. Whenever I wanted to watch euphonias—no matter what the time of day—all I had to do was wait under a tree that had mistletoe in it. The little birds came by, in family parties of five or six as a rule, the "scrubs" in one flock, the "yellowthroats" in another. The call notes of the busy birds sounded conversational. When a Scrub Euphonia sang, the syllables sounded like *see-see-see, dewd-see* to me. A song that I heard on the Mesa de Llera on January 13, 1949, sounded like *tsew, diddily*.

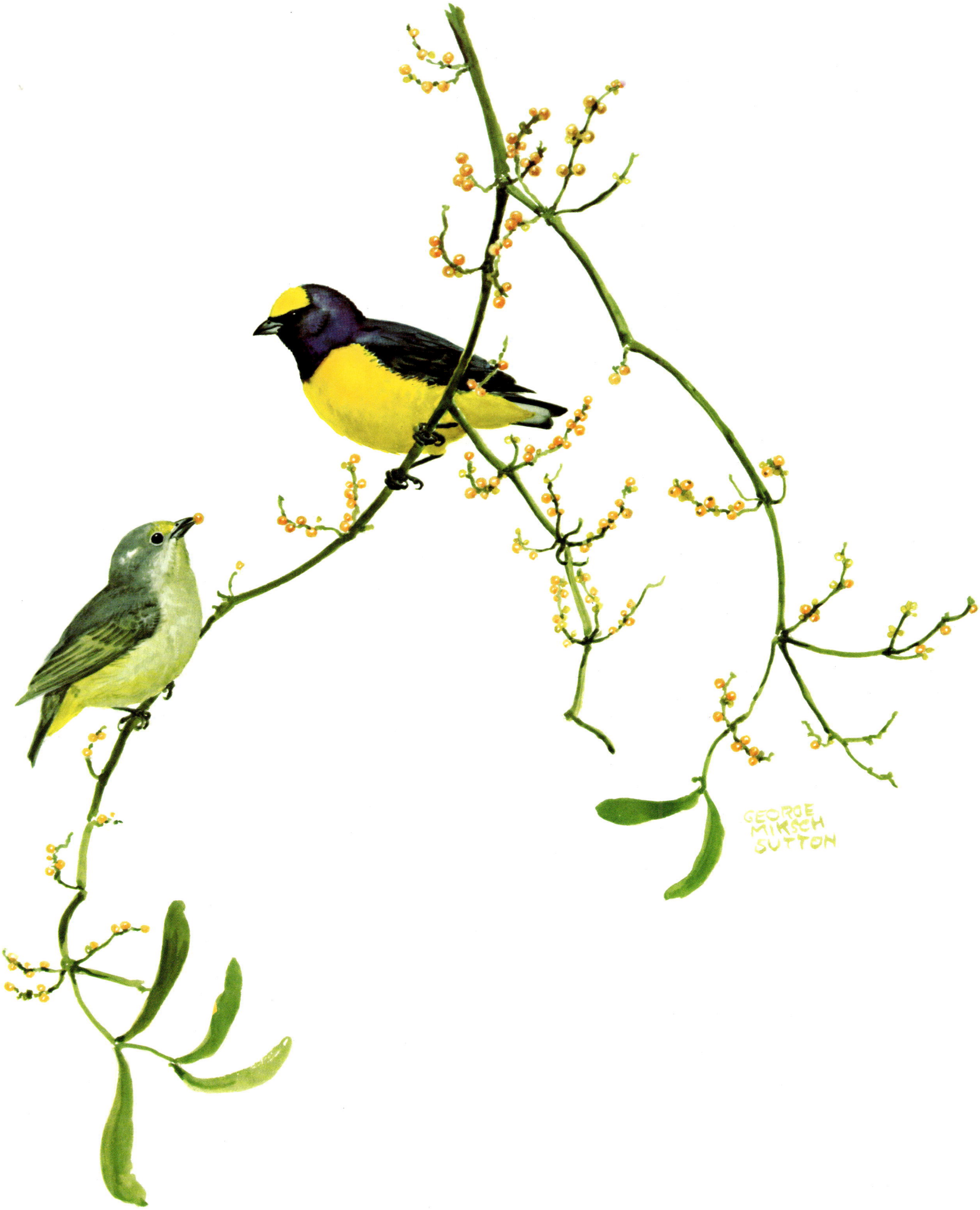
GEORGE
MIKSCH
SUTTON

RED-THROATED ANT TANAGER

One of the most elusive birds that Ernest P. Edwards, Robert B. Lea, and I observed during our short stay in southwestern Tamaulipas in the latter half of May, 1947, was the Red-throated Ant Tanager *(Habia fuscicauda)*. I say elusive because we had so much trouble seeing the bird. Its rough, chattered scolding and occasional bursts of rhythmic song we'd hear off in the brush, but seeing it meant leaving the trail and sneaking through the barbed *huapilla*—tick habitat—and this we avoided whenever possible. Most birds of the valley were breeding, but the ant tanagers seemed to be going about not in pairs but in flocks. When, on May 25, I collected two females from the same flock and found that each had been laying eggs, I suspected that the species might be nesting semicolonially. I looked hard for nests, but in vain.

The two female specimens and a male collected a day or so earlier served as models. I wanted to show in detail at least one characteristic plant of the tanager's habitat, so decided on a climbing cactus that grew at the edge of a trail about half a mile from camp. The final trip to this outdoor studio proved to be something of an expedition, for I had to carry an easel (made from saplings tied together), a collapsible stool, the big drawing board and sheet of paper, the battered Fuertes paint-box, a jar of halazoned water, etc., not to mention the tanager specimens, the male already a prepared skin, the two females unskinned. Accompanying me was an utterly nondescript, undernourished, small white dog, whose general appearance was so cadaverous that we had nicknamed him Casi Muerto (Nearly Dead). Where Casi Muerto had come from we had no idea. A born pariah, he had hung around camp; we had made the mistake of giving him something to eat; so he had become ours.

Telling Casi Muerto to go home while I was on my way to the painting spot did no good, no good at all. Warned by a rough voice that he would be shot and thrown to the *zopilotes*, he put his thin tail between his thin hind legs, turned sadly, and hurriedly retraced his steps; but around the first bend in the trail he decided to join the expedition again, *zopilotes* or no. I should have stopped, put paraphernalia down, and given the wretched dog the switching of his life, but this I did not do.

So the painting got started. The sky was overcast. There was no bothersome glare from the big sheet of white paper. My stool was in a perfectly bare spot, well away from the thicket and its ticks. But the mosquitoes, rejoicing because there was no sun, were savage. Knowing that slapping was just what they wanted—for slapping brought that good red blood to within easy drilling distance—I mashed them decorously, giving each one undivided attention, muttering indecorously as I flicked the dead insect away. Most of their biting they did on my knees where the cloth was thin and stretched tight.

Removing mosquitoes from the halazoned water was boresome. Picking up a pencil or brush dropped while mashing a mosquito also was boresome. Sharpening a lead broken because the pencil had been dropped while mashing a mosquito was very boresome. Worst of all was that ill-starred moment when I mashed a mosquito, dropped a pencil, picked the pencil up to find its lead broken, reached for the pocket knife that had been put carefully down near the open paint-box, only to find paint-box, pocket knife, spare brushes, and extra erasers *all* under Casi Muerto, who had curled up and gone to sleep on them.

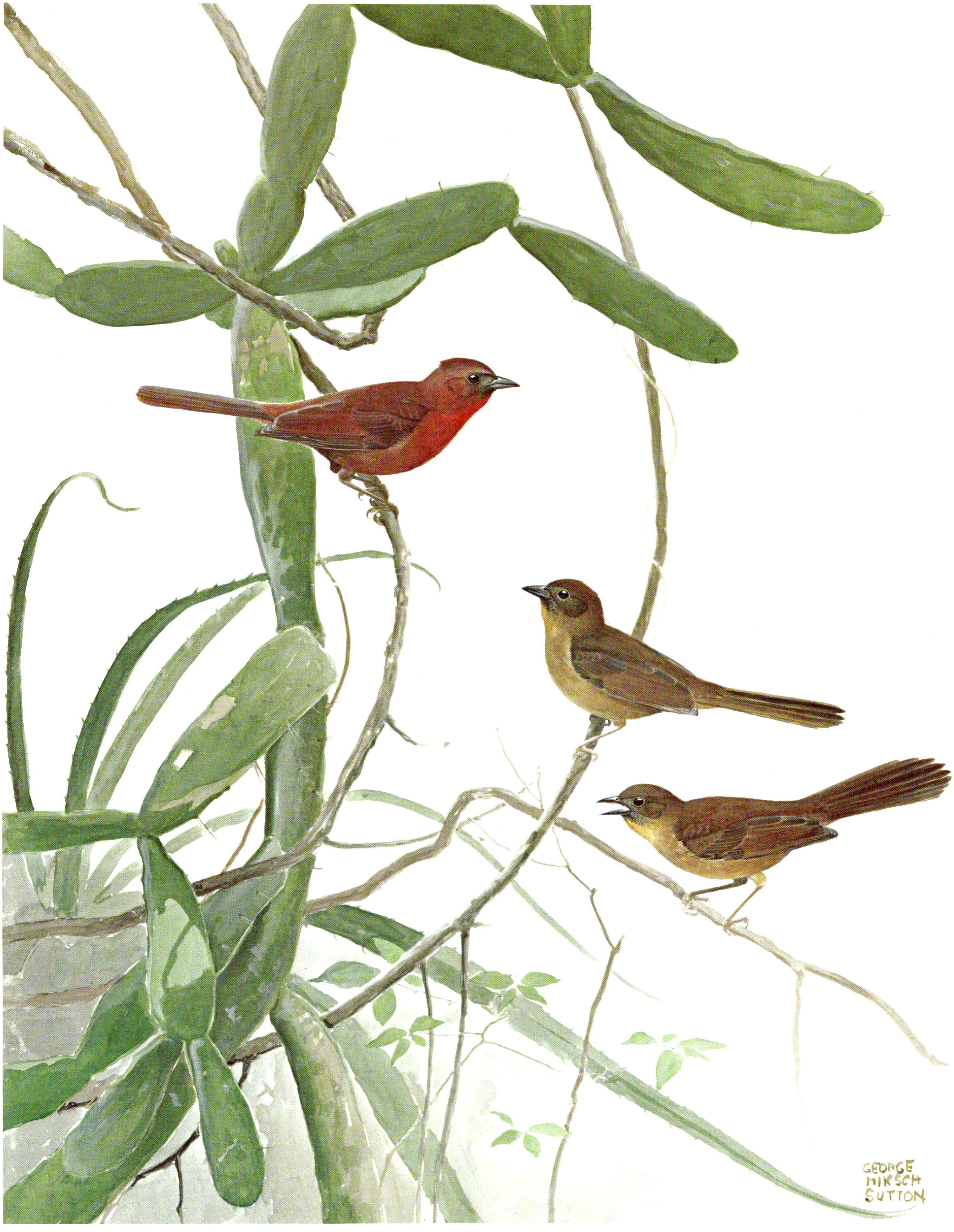
GEORGE
MIKSCH
SUTTON

BLACK-HEADED SALTATOR

The saltators, or jumpers, are large New World finches that are not—so far as I have observed—in any way notable for their jumping. With two of the three Mexican species, the big Black-headed Saltator *(Saltator atriceps)*, which is fully 10 inches long, and the smaller Grayish Saltator *(S. coerulescens)*, which is about 8 inches long, I have become well acquainted. Both of these range northward in eastern Mexico as far as southern Tamaulipas and eastern San Luis Potosí, but in western Mexico the northern limits of the Black-headed species are in central Guerrero, whereas those of the Grayish species are in Sinaloa. The Black-headed's southern limits are in Panama, those of the Grayish in northern Argentina. The scientific name of the third Mexican species, the Buff-throated Saltator *(S. maximus)*, is misleading, for the bird is only about 8 inches long. Its northern limits are in Veracruz, its southern limits in Brazil.

In southern Tamaulipas and eastern San Luis Potosí the Black-headed and Grayish species have about the same habitat, though the former seems to prefer heavy woods along streams, the latter, brushy areas. Along the Río Sabinas I could count on hearing both—the clearly enunciated *chuck-pree* or *chucker-pree* (with rising inflection) of the Grayish, and the strange *cheek*, *chu-eek*, *churr* and rattling chatter of the Black-headed. The most characteristic call of the Grayish, as transliterated above, seems to be a true song; but the expostulations of the Black-headed are so noisy and so wholly unmusical as to seem like almost anything but song.

Near our house at the Rancho Rinconada the Black-headed Saltator was common, especially in clumps of bamboo near the river. The handsome bird squeaked-up readily, often responding with chips of alarm followed by an incredible *chicker, chacker, chucker-ur-ur-ur-ur-ur* that called to mind the scolding of a big squirrel. These "songs" sometimes made me laugh, especially when two or three birds sounded off together or when one of them, after flying up a way, performed in mid-air with wings flopping and legs dangling, descending slowly to the bamboo tangle while continuing the odd noises. *Demonstrations of this sort can't possibly be of use to the bird*, I'd say to myself; *they're overdone and preposterous*. Then would come the calm after my little personal storm: *What would this lovely spot be without them? What would I be without them?*

Along the Sabinas we failed to find a Black-headed Saltator's nest, but near the lovely fall on the Río Naranjo in San Luis Potosí, between May 17 and 28, 1947, we found three unfinished nests in vine-covered shrubbery a few feet from the ground. They were bulky, sprawling, thin-walled, and rather deeply cupped. On May 28 all were finished, ready for the first eggs.

My drawing shows a male bird in a shrub called the *pata de vaca* or cowhoof plant, from the oddly shaped leaves. I made the painting on April 22, 1941, near Gómez Farías, Tamaulipas.

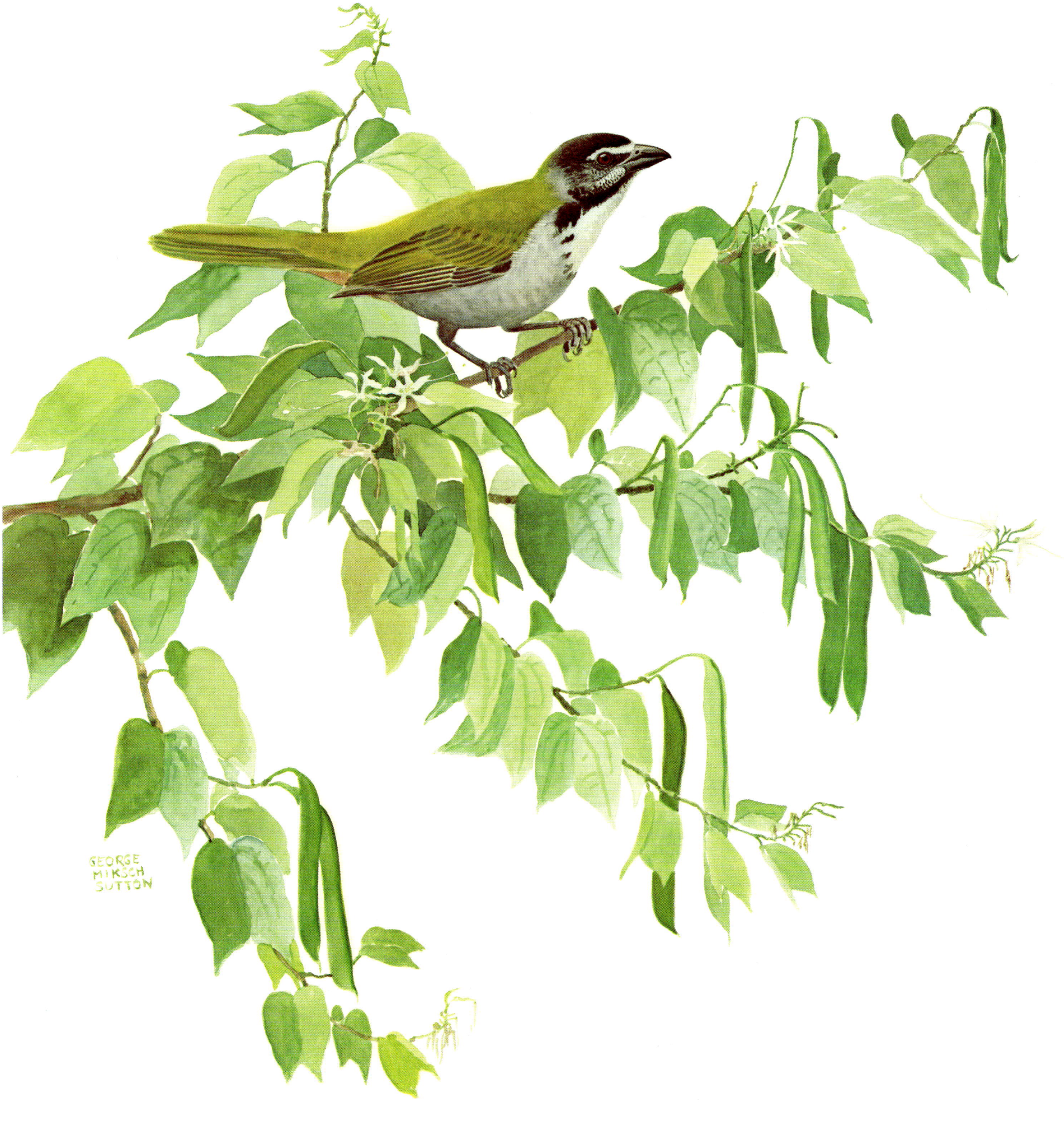
GEORGE
MIKSCH
SUTTON

BLUE BUNTING

A fairly common, though not very conspicuous, bird of Mexican lowlands and lesser foothills is the Blue Bunting *(Cyanocompsa parellina)*, a somewhat chunky finch about 5 inches long. At a distance the male appears to be black except for the forget-me-not blue of the forehead, cheeks, rump, and lesser wing coverts; the female, warm brown all over, a little paler on the throat and belly than elsewhere. In the hand the black of the male is a rich, deep blue.

The species inhabits thickets, brushy woods, and old fields. It does not seem to mind dry areas, often being found in thorny vegetation well away from water. In the coastal plain of eastern Mexico I have often seen and heard it while walking along a road through monotonous chaparral. Its song is simple but cheery, a syllable something like *chwing* or *chweeng* five or six times repeated rather rapidly. My field-notes concerning the song carry me back to March 2, 1941, when our party of four drove from Linares, Nuevo León, to the remote hill village of Galeana via the spectacular Cañon de Iturbide and its unbelievable road, some lengthy one-way stretches of which had been hacked from the base of a vast cliff. That road was tortuous and difficult, to say the least. I recall especially a sharp curve, a dip, and a sudden confrontation with armed troops, all in quick succession, that gave me the feeling that "this was it." The troops, most of them afoot, let us pass, but not a single man smiled.

The above does not sound much like a report on bird observation, I know, but sharp curves, dips, and confrontations are part of ornithology.

At Linares we were near the northern tip of the Blue Bunting's range in eastern Mexico. In western Mexico the northern limits are in central Sinaloa. The species is characteristic of both eastern and western coastal slopes of Mexico and Central America as far southward as Nicaragua. It is fairly common near the sacred cenote at Chichén Itzá, Yucatán, and in thickets bordering canefields in Colima. It usually goes about in pairs, even in winter, though at that season it may mingle with small birds of other species. Its song, though never very noticeable, declares its presence, but seeing the singer may require persistent stalking. Along a road there is always a chance that singing will stop at one side, a brown bird followed by a black will fly across, and singing will resume on the other side.

My drawing, made on May 20, 1947, along the Río Sabinas in southwestern Tamaulipas, shows a pair of Blue Buntings and a "wild tomato" plant of the genus *Solanum*. The season had been dreadfully dry before our party's arrival that year, but during our stay it rained often. So often, in fact, that as I painted the buntings I was obliged to rush to and from nightshade plant and shed several times. Moving easel, paints, stool, drawing-board, etc. wasn't accomplished by pushing some button. I couldn't even boil things down enough to move them with one trip. I did learn, however, that I could dip my brush in water that accumulated in big leaves during showers, and thus obviate the need for that abominable glass of halazoned water. Water in the leaves had not been sterilized, of course, but I figured that anything fresh from God's heaven would be safe.

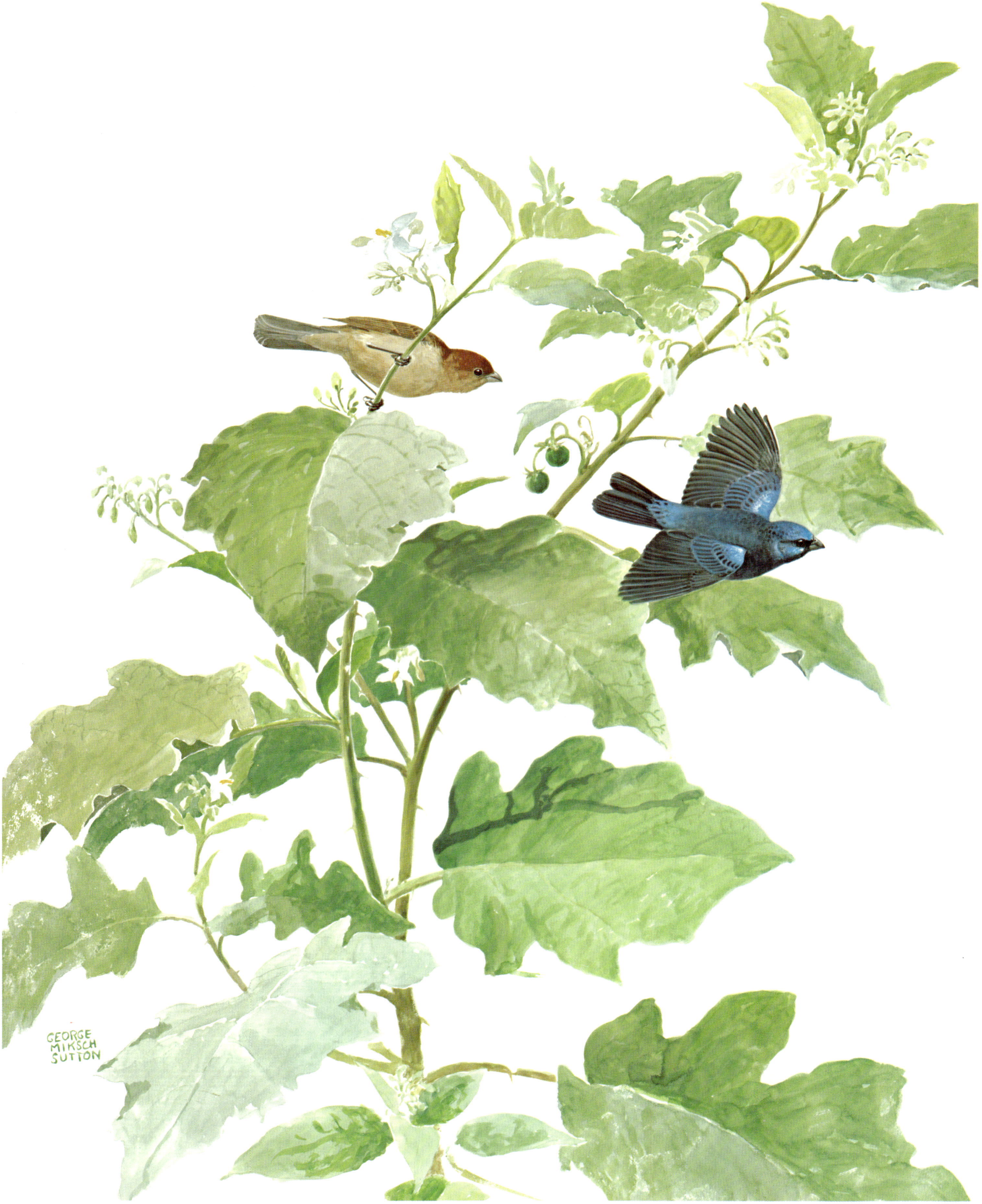
GEORGE
MIKSCH
SUTTON

A WORD FROM THE AUTHOR

On most of my trips to Mexico between 1938 and 1975 I have devoted considerable time to drawing birds. As a rule, the work has not been easy, since I have had to fit it into a busy program of field observation, specimen preparation, and note-taking—not to mention the job of moving from place to place, establishing camp, etc. But always it has given me inner satisfaction, for I have felt that through it I might be making my own special contribution to ornithology.

The drawings made on my first expedition to Mexico (1938) were all done on 11 x 14-inch sheets of fairly smooth two-ply Strathmore watercolor bond. On that expedition John B. Semple, Thomas D. Burleigh, and I visited the states of Coahuila, Nuevo León, and Tamaulipas. Most of the drawings were of birds' heads, but those of the Bat Falcon (*Falco albigularis*), Green Kingfisher (*Chloroceryle americana*), Elegant Trogon (*Trogon elegans*), and Crimson-collared Grosbeak (*Rhodothraupis celaeno*) were of the whole bird. These four were reproduced in color, the falcon, kingfisher, and grosbeak in *The Wilson Bulletin* and in my book *Mexican Birds* (1951), the trogon in *Mexican Birds* and in the *Proceedings* of the 13th International Ornithological Congress, which met in 1938 at Rouen, France.

On my second trip to Mexico (1939), there was not much time for drawing. That year Semple, Burleigh, and I went much farther south, reaching the states of San Luis Potosí, Hidalgo, México, Morelos, Puebla, and Veracruz. At the village of Las Vigas, Veracruz, I spent several days with one of my graduate students, Frederick W. Loetscher, Jr. The drawings made on that trip again were on sheets of two-ply Strathmore, each measuring 11 x 14 inches. The most notable of them was of the head of an Emerald Toucanet (*Aulacorhynchus prasinus*)—a drawing reproduced in color in *The Wilson Bulletin* and later in *Mexican Birds*.

When, in the early spring of 1941, Olin Sewall Pettingill, Jr. and I decided to invade the hill country of southwestern Tamaulipas with graduate students, collecting and photographic equipment, formalin and alcohol for herpetological specimens, and glass slides for blood-smears, I sensed that the time had come for a grander performance from me. So the sheets of Strathmore that I bought were the biggest I could get (about 22 x 29 inches), and I had a light-weight plywood drawing-board of slightly larger dimensions sawed out for me.

Several of the drawings made that spring are reproduced here. A few of them—especially that of the Military Macaw (*Ara militaris*)—were badly overcrowded as a result of my decision to show the birds life-size. The botanical parts of each picture were carefully considered before I started drawing. As a rule I did the plants direct from life—that is, without cutting them and bringing them indoors.

Mexican boys, puzzled but interested, watch the artist at work. Photograph by Robert B. Lea

Camp along the Río Sabinas in the spring of 1947. Photograph by Ernest P. Edwards

So big sheets of paper, big drawing-board, and the old Fuertes paintbox were part of every trip to Mexico from then on. Such luggage sometimes posed problems. In 1947, when I flew to Monterrey and traveled from there to Ciudad Mante, Tamaulipas, by bus, where I met Ernest P. Edwards and Robert B. Lea, I decided that what I had with me were *impedimenta* indeed, for finding a place for the big drawing-board and the envelope containing paper was difficult. Anyone who has traveled by "local" bus in Mexico need not be told of the chickens, turkeys, pigs, goats, dogs, and produce that are crammed in between, under, and above the passengers. My seat-mate on that whole journey was a fine young *paisano* whose imagination supplied what my sentences in Spanish lacked, who became more and more friendly as I pointed out spots at which I had been afield, and who finally, even despite protest from me, undid a big, well-wrapped box in order to show me an amazing assortment of crystal figurines that he was taking to his wife and children. I could not help wondering where in Monterrey he had found that elegant "glass menagerie." He must have paid a good deal for it.

Some drawings made on every expedition have been crude field sketches—like one of a Plumbeous Kite (*Ictinia plumbea*) made on May 22, 1947—designed to emphasize an important point or two but not intended to be a work of art. This particular sketch proved that a finished life-size drawing that I had made in 1941 was entirely correct in showing the crossed wingtips extending well beyond the tip of the tail; but with equal force it called attention to a sort of crest above the eye, a hump in the fore part of the crown plumage, that the earlier drawing failed to show. Was head-shape in the earlier drawing wrong? Probably not. The fluffed-out body plumage and "forehead hump" in the field sketch were indicative of complete ease, full stomach, and relaxation. The bird in my earlier drawing was at ease, but not to the point of lethargy and drowsiness. Its body plumage was not fluffed out. Had I drawn a "forehead hump" on a bird whose body plumage was not fluffed out, I might have erred.

For years I have been shouting from the housetops that the most authentic bird drawings are made not from photographs, mounted specimens, or scientific skins, but from living models. I have not meant to say that drawings made in some other way should be consigned to the trash can; nor have I meant to derogate the basing of a final drawing on crude sketches made in the field. Thoughtfully re-worded, what I have said should make clear that in my opinion *my* best drawings have been made, literally from start to finish, with living models two or three feet from my face, right hand, and drawing-board. Actually, I have not made more than fifty or so drawings in just that way, but among them are a few that thrill me whenever I look at them. Let this not be considered self-praise; it is merely an honest statement about work done in a certain way.

As a youngster seven or eight years old I must have sensed that living models were important. In those Nebraska days about the turn of the century I made crude crayon redbird, bluebird, and blackbird drawings which I took from door to door in a little wagon, selling them at a penny apiece.

El Salto, the beautiful waterfall along the Río Naranjo in San Luis Potosí, as it was in the spring of 1947. Photograph by Ernest P. Edwards

Dwain Warner holds a freshly-shot Boat-billed Heron specimen while Sutton draws it. Photograph by Olin Sewall Pettingill Jr.

Indulgent neighbors actually bought them. With the money I obtained long, rubbery strips of black "likkerish," a confection my sister Dorothy and I doted on. Came the day when she and I were taken to a State Fair in Lincoln where we were to see a huge "Mississippi Catfish" in a tank barely big enough to hold it, a stuffed rattlesnake lord knows how long, cattle, horses, and pigs combed and brushed to the nines, and a huge blue-ribboned rooster of what H. H. Munro would have called "Barred Plymouth Rock persuasion" with whom I fell hopelessly in love. I do not recall arguing with anyone over my desire to stay with that rooster, but I do recall finding paper and pencil and drawing, drawing, drawing until I had recorded my impressions of the awesome fowl. When a man who saw me at work asked how close I was to completing it, he stayed at my elbow, held the finished picture in his hands, and announced that he wanted to buy it. I did not like to part with it, but the idea of being paid salved my feelings, so off the picture went, and into my pocket went *a whole dime*.

During the following four or five years my drawings were made mostly from dead birds, from memories of living birds, and from imagination, but never, oddly enough, from pictures of birds. An unbelievable roll of pencil drawings made in Oregon when I was ten years old includes one of a "Red Wing" that had an extra bone in each leg. Where this weird concept came from I do not know, but it runs in my mind that it was related to an important discovery, namely that what I had been calling a bird's knee flexed in wholly the wrong way, that this "knee" was actually the heel or ankle, that the real knee was hidden up among the plumage of the underparts.

I was about fifteen years old, and in Texas, when the idea struck me full force that really authentic drawings should be made direct from living birds. On April 22, 1913, I made a direct-from-life portrait of a stub-tailed Roadrunner (*Geococcyx californianus*) that I was rearing. Somehow I never threw this drawing away. I still have it. It was reproduced as a halftone in *The Wilson Bulletin* a few years ago (1968, Vol. 80, p. 32).

From the above paragraphs readers might logically assume that every drawing reproduced in this book was made directly from a living model. Alas, most of them were not. That of the Red-crowned Parrot was, from start to finish. My model that time was not a pet, but, being unable to fly, it was quite content to "stay put" while I drew it. Many of the drawings were made with free-flying models not far away (e.g., the two Fan-tailed Warblers, the Northern Pygmy Owl, and the White-eared Hummingbirds), but most of them were done with a freshly-collected specimen in hand at a table indoors or at camp. Botanical parts of pictures

The Río Sabinas along which many of the drawings reproduced in this book were made. Photographed on April 10, 1955, by Dale A. Zimmerman

I usually did with the paper propped up on an easel, but doing the birds required bringing the drawing-board down to horizontal. Being able to spread the wings, open the bill, and move the legs and toes of a specimen was very important. Never did I try wiring a specimen into a desired position, but I sometimes pinned a spread wing out so as to depict its markings properly.

Working directly from life can be very difficult, even nerve-racking. A drowsy owl may remain motionless for hours at a stretch by day but "come to life" at night. Well-fed young birds make good models, for they quiet down and stay that way until they become hungry. Adult birds caught in a net may beat themselves silly if caged and hang themselves if tethered. Often I have had success holding a captive bird in my left hand while painting with my right. Wrapping a bird snugly in cloth to keep it from flapping its wings and kicking forces it to be quiet while its head is being drawn, but this method does not help with recording over-all shape.

In May, 1973, at the Hacienda el Cóbano in Colima, southwestern Mexico, I announced that I wanted living models for my painting if possible. Angel Lara, the capable man in charge, learned of a tame Chachalaca (*Ortalis vetula*) in the neighborhood and had the bird brought to me. It was a demure creature that submitted meekly enough to being wrapped in an old towel while I started to draw its head. When I started penciling-in the body, however, I was at a loss, for I could not let my model go, I had no cage, and—worst of all—the bird had only the tattered basal third of its tail. Evidently, despite its docility, times had been hard for it. My friend Emma Messerly offered to hold the Chachalaca for me, and hold it she did—literally by the hour. My drawing of the head was acceptable, but somehow the picture as a whole did not come off. I had placed the head so low on the big sheet that by the time I added the body there wasn't room for the whole tail.

Wondering if foreshortening body and tail might solve the problem, I thanked Emma and suggested that she take a rest. I put the wrapped-up Chachalaca on the table near me, and tried redrawing in such a way as to get the whole, properly feathered tail on the paper. Time dragged. My spirits sank. My model took it all gracefully enough, though if ever in its life it did any wondering, it must have done some then.

Quite without making a sound came the hacienda's three dogs, all well mannered but curious. The largest sniffed at the Chachalaca, sending the poor bird into understandable panic. Out of its wrapping it burst with a squawk. With wings thumping frantically it made off, while pencils, brushes, and erasers flew, tumbler of water toppled, and paintbox crashed to the floor. The dogs gave chase. Exasperated, I roared, but the dogs interpreted the sound as exhortation and charged with vigor. Within seconds feathers were in the air, the dogs were nosing the cornered bird, and the artist was whacking the dogs. Fortunately the Chachalaca came through it all unhurt.

When Angel Lara learned of the incident he said to me, "Those dogs would never have hurt that bird." What he meant was, of course, that the dogs wouldn't have *intended* to hurt the bird; what they intended was to catch it for me. Alas, how often do attempts to communicate fail!